Judi Letters

Judi Letters

(A collection of ancestral recollections of early families related to the McDonalds and Lindseys of Lauderdale County, Alabama.)

By

William Lindsey McDonald & Thomas G. McDonald

Judi Letters

Published by

Bluewater Publications

Copyright © 2008 Bluewater Publications

All rights reserved.

www.BluewaterPublications.com

Table of Contents

Forward

Recently, the papers of William Lindsey McDonald have been archived as part of the Collier Library on the campus of the University of North Alabama. The attached collection of our family, through the lines of our dear mother, Pauline Lindsey McDonald, have been reassembled in order to depict a heritage that otherwise may have been lost on younger generations of our family.

Thanks & Recognition

Valuable assistance was rendered by Tom McDonald, brother of the author, in researching and compiling materials for this publication. Born in Florence, Alabama, Tom McDonald is a retired educator. His interests are many, including carpentry, reading, old tractors and gardening. He and his wife, Margo, have lived in Florence all of their lives and now reside just off the historic Natchez Trace in Northwest Alabama with their dogs, Ned and Sam. They enjoy camping, hiking in the Smoky Mountains and spending time with their two children, grandchildren and extended family. They are actively involved in their church and community.

Dedication

This book is published as a token of appreciation for all the love and family care lavished on her brothers by our only sister, Virginia Lindsey. Words are simply inadequate to express the gratitude we feel for the love and devotion she showered on her six, often inappreciative, brothers throughout all these years.

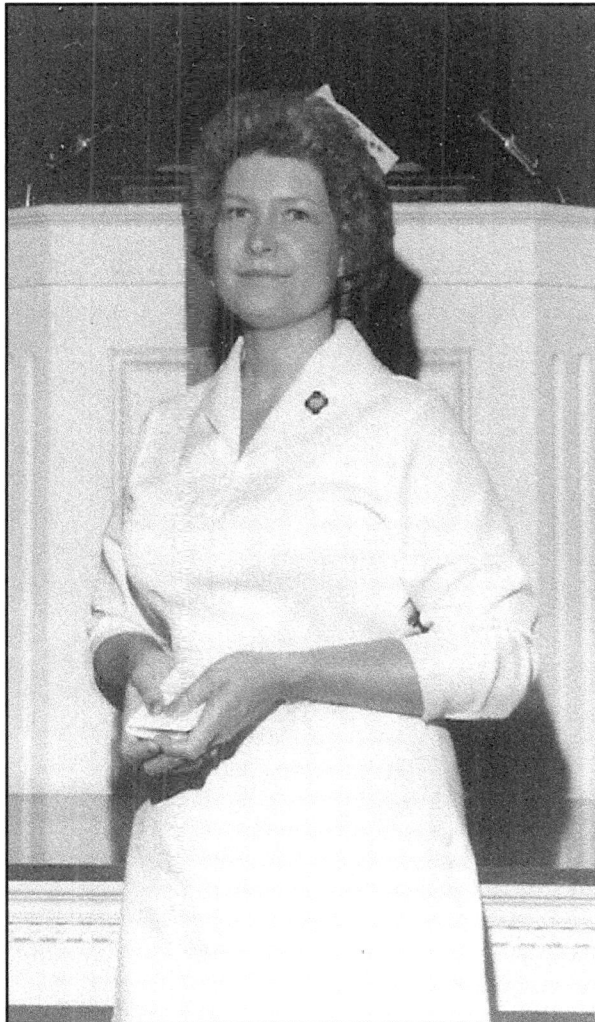

Introduction

This work is a compilation of a series of letters written years ago to Judi Lindsey. Judi is one of Uncle Claude Lindsey's daughters who lived in Montgomery. She knew absolutely nothing about her father's family and had no contact with any of us. Her daddy had suggested that she get in touch with me to find out about her family tree. As a result of our conversation, I wrote her this series of letters over the years.

I had intended, through the years, to write a history of the Johnson side of the family, which is on my mother's side. Thankfully, I was able to complete the work on the McDonalds and the Lindseys, but I never found the time I had hoped for to write about the Johnson side of the family, which goes back even earlier than any of the records that I have. I am now in the nursing home and realize that my time and available resources are pretty well running low. So, my brother Tom and I have decided to go ahead and merge these letters that I wrote to Judi and use them as a text for what we plan to publish as a manner of recording that side of the family. We are in the process of collecting old pictures. Hopefully, we can use these photographs in what we will ultimately publish on the Johnson side of our family.

My mother's mother was Lucy Lavania Johnson. Her mother and father were Franklin Pierce Johnson and Mary Ellender McCuan Johnson. We have looked through the Lindsey papers and found there was so much not included in the Lindsey book that Tom and I mutually agreed to include this additional information on the Lindseys in this publication.

The Lindseys are a very interesting side of our family in that they go back to Scotland. The first of the Lindseys came to this country as an ordained minister in Virginia. We are now in the process of placing a headstone at the gravesite of our great-great-great-grandfather, John L. Lindsey, who was a veteran of the Revolutionary War. (See "Soldier Boy In Blue" in Appendix 5.) The grave is located in what is known as Cooper Cemetery on Cooper Creek in the community of Cypress Inn, Tennessee. After this marker is placed, this will pretty well mark the graves of all the early people of our family who came here from Virginia and South Carolina in the early settlement of northwest Alabama.

Our mother's grandmother, Martha Johnson, was a Nichols whose father was a Methodist minister who rode a circuit. They came from the area around what is now Birmingham. They wound up in Wayne County, Tennessee, and from there into the northwest corner of Alabama.

Our grandmother Lindsey's maternal grandmother was Sarah Bernard. Her grandfather was Abner Alloway Strange, who was a veteran of the American Revolution. He was with General Greene who was with General Washington at Yorktown when he received the surrender of the British Army. He wrote in his application for a pension that he saw and knew both General Washington and General Nathaniel Greene. These papers can be found in Fluvanna County, Virginia. I spent considerable time up there working with the papers of our Bernard and Strange families. Abner Strange moved from Fluvanna County, Virginia, in 1824 and settled in Limestone County, Alabama, in a place known as Salem in the northwest corner of this county.

Abner's daughter Sarah was my great-great-great-grandmother. She was married to Charles M. Bernard. He came from quite an influential family in Fluvanna County, Virginia, which is right at the base of the mountain on which Thomas Jefferson built his home, Monticello. I spent considerable time in Fluvanna County and was blessed to have been introduced to an elderly lady who was a historian of Fluvanna County, and she was distantly related to us through the Stranges and Bernards. I wish now I could record her name, but I can't recall it at the moment.

The Strange and Bernard cemeteries are still intact on the old plantations. The people there were so kind. When they found out that I was coming, they even mowed the pathway to these old family cemeteries. I actually found the graves of the mother and father of Abner Strange as well as Charles M. Bernard's immediate family grave.

This little collection of Judi letters includes that side of our family. Heretofore, we have not attempted to pass on information we have collected over some 60 years. I hope you will find these papers of some interest and that you will hold them in your collection so that your children and your children's children will know something about our ancestors and where we came from.

William Lindsey McDonald
Florence, Alabama

Citation

HONORARY DEGREE

Doctor of Humane Letters

Conferred upon

WILLIAM LINDSEY MCDONALD

By the

UNIVERSITY OF NORTH ALABAMA

May 13, 2006

You are known throughout the Shoals for your exhaustive knowledge of this area's history. We are proud today to include you in the history of the University of North Alabama as we honor an alumnus and friend. You have dedicated much of your life to researching and collecting historical information about the Shoals area. Without doubt, your extensive research and personal collection of historica documents are beyond compare. You continue to amaze the citizens of northwest Alabama with your wealth of historical knowledge, and particularly, you have rendered valuable service to your alma mater over the years with your research and documentation on the establishment of the University of North Alabama in 1830. You are an analyst, an author of prestigious books and articles, a devoted historian and researcher, and a gentleman.

We also give tribute for your thirty-eight years of military service to our country, including your U.S. Army tours in World War II and the Korean War and your work at the Pentagon. We applaud your personal convictions, your faith, and your willingness to assist persons or organizations who seek to learn more about the past. We are pleased to add this honor to the numerous awards and commendations you have received over the years. It is with Great pleasure, therefore, that the University of North Alabama, by the unanimous action of its Board of Trustee, confers upon you the honorary degree of Doctor of Humane Letters, with all the rights and privileges thereunto appertaining.

Letters

Dear Cousin Judi: June 5, 1977

Words cannot convey the excitement of receiving your letter. I have longed for
the opportunity of knowing Claude's children. It has really bothered me
thinking that we would go through life and not know one another. I tried some
time ago to contact Claude, Jr. But guess he did not get the letter (mailed to
where I thought he worked.) I have planned to look up your sister, Lucy, the
next time I'm in Oklahoma. Her name is so beautiful. That was Mama Lindsey's
name.

Judi, what a shame you did not know our grandparents. We knew them as Papa
and Mama Lindsey. She was a jolly and religious little lady who knew all about
her ancestors that she had learned from her grandmother. I copied down many
of her stories. (Some of them have been published in papers, which I shall send
you copies later on.) Papa Lindsey was a quarter-Indian. He had strange ways
and most people did not understand. But I did. He was my idol, my hero, my
ideal of a man and father and grandfather. Papa was very religious. He was
straight, like his Indian ancestors, had a flock of the whitest hair I have ever
known. He ran a grocery store. I worked for him from the time I could walk
until I went to the Army. He and I remained the best of friends until the day he
died.

I'll tell you more about these two wonderful people later. I'm sending a few
copies of our genealogy to get you started. I have several large notebooks
crammed full of family data. I shall send you copies of records piece by piece, so
that I can try and tell you something about each generation. Mama Lindsey
came from an aristocratic old Virginia family, who settled in Jamestown in 1619
from the Orkney Island in Scotland. I can trace one side of her family back to
1148 AD. However, in some cases between 1148 and 1500, I have names of
grandfather and grandson (with the father missing). These came from Scotland

land records that had only the names of the ones who inherited titled property. But they are our line of the family.

You just must plan to visit me. I have the old family Bible from Virginia, plus old pictures, and even the big bed from our ancestral home in Lauderdale County. In fact, you would not believe some of the things I have (even the long beard of our great-great-grandfather, Nelson McCuan). Mama Lindsey's oldest sister, Grand-aunt Maggie, willed me most of all the family history and artifacts.

I have run out of space for this time. Please write and tell me about yourself and family. (I have a list of all you children. But I need your birth dates, and who you married, and your addresses.) Again, you just don't know how happy I am to hear from you (and how exciting that you are interested in the family). I have lots of material on all sides and shall be more than delighted to share everything with you.

Dick

Dear Judi: June 12, 1977

I received your letter yesterday. Hope you don't mind, but I had to share it with
Aunt Lura. We are all anxious to meet you and are looking forward to your visit.
First, because you are family and someone we have never seen. Second, there is
so much to tell you, and show you, and places you just must see. We can see all
the sites where our family lived and died. I have so few who are really
interested. In fact, you'll find that I have several tours lined up for you already.
And we'll be expecting you — as you said, "before the summer is over." Really
hope Lucy can come too. (We are marking the 3rd week in July on our calendars
— Lucy's vacation.) By the way, Aunt Lura remembers that Lucy was born at
Maxwell AFB. She was there not long after her birth.

I'm sending two more generations on Papa Lindsey's side. Adrian Leonard
Lindsey Sr. {see Appendix 7} was Papa's father. He was an old soldier of the
Confederate Army. We have a large oil portrait of him in uniform. It hangs
upstairs in my home. He fought four years in Company C of the 27th Alabama
Infantry. I have his war record that I copied in Washington. He enlisted in
Florence. When he was discharged after the war, he walked all the way from
Demopolis, Alabama, to Waterloo. Waterloo is about 30 miles from Florence.
There is where Papa Lindsey was born and lived until he came to Florence about
1900. Adrian was wounded in the Battle of Baton Rouge, Louisiana. A caisson
ran over him on the battlefield and broke his arm at the elbow and his leg at the
knee. He was crippled for the remaining years of his life. He lived to be 89 years
of age and lived with Mama and Papa Lindsey for the last few years before he
died. He is buried in "Soldier's Rest," the Confederate Cemetery in Florence.

Of Papa's family, I can only remember Aunt Lula. She lived in Waterloo until
several years before she died in Tyronzee, Arkansas. We would all load up in
Papa's truck and visit her. She looked like an Indian, dark and straight hair with
high cheekbones, and a dark complexion. My mother and Uncle Nelson had her
hair and complexion. You will be amazed at how much like an Indian your Uncle
Nelson looks. In fact, my wife, Dorothy, used him as a model for her Indian

13

paintings at the Indian Mound Museum. Papa Lindsey was the youngest child. Lula, Calvin, and Hunter were born before the Civil War. And all but Aunt Lula were dead before my day. Papa Lindsey and I placed a marker on Uncle Hunter's grave in Wright, Alabama, not too many years before Papa's death.

Papa's mother, Martha Jane Higgins, was a half Indian. She died when Papa was but 10 years of age. She is buried near Waterloo on top of a high hill with her family, the Higginses. Papa and I would often go there and visit her grave. We also made trips to the old family homestead on Manbone Creek near Waterloo, and Papa would point out the big rock where his mother would wash her clothes at the edge of the creek.

The next generation I'm sending this time is that of the Higgins family. Josiah was the father of Martha Jane Higgins Lindsey, Papa's mother. He was a rather progressive farmer for his day and age (as you will notice in my notes on the record). Papa's first cousin, Jimmy Haines, owned the old homestead when I was a boy. We would go there with Papa and stand in awe at the big house built by slaves and play on the long porches that circled the two-storied house. Papa would always point out the solid rock cover for the well; slaves had cut a hole in the rock for the buckets to be let down in the well. I did not know any of Josiah's children. Most of them are buried near Papa's mother. But Papa loved them best of all his people. He would talk of Uncle Dock, Uncle Richard, and Aunt Catherine mostly. I would carry Papa to Waterloo in his old days, and we would spend a whole day visiting the children of his aunts and uncles — Papa's first cousins.

As I have already told you, Great-Grandmother Higgins was a full-blooded Chickasaw Indian. Census records show she was born in Alabama before Alabama became a state. Papa used to laugh about my big head and say that it came from the Roundheads, whom he claimed his Grandmother Higgins was. This didn't mean much to me until a few years ago. While in Washington, I read that a strange round-headed race of Indians lived on Seven Mile Island in the Tennessee River in Alabama. (Seven Mile Island is near Waterloo, Alabama.)

14

These Indians were called Roundheads and were of the Chickasaw race. However, it is thought that originally they were of a race descended from the Choctaw. After Charlotte's death (Charlotte was her Christian name; her Indian name was Chealty), Great-Grandpa Higgins married the second time to a lady by the first name of Kate (he referred to her as Kate B. Higgins in his will that I have in my archives).

The old Higgins' homestead and farm is now under the great Pickwick Lake. When they took the land from Cousin Jimmy Haines, he never forgave TVA and would refuse to look at the lake where the old place was. It was a rich bottomland that grew the highest corn in the farms around Waterloo. (This happened about 1936 when Pickwick Dam was built by TVA.)

Josiah Higgins' father was Alexander Higgins (born 1790 and died 1830). This is as far as I have been able to go on the Higgins line, but only because I haven't had the time to try. I bet we would be able to find a lot about them.

Next time, I'll continue with Papa's line (Lindseys and Sharps).

Judi, you don't realize it, but you have inherited your interest in the family from your grandmother Lindsey. She was such a remarkable little woman. She loved the family and knew everything about all the generations on all sides. Mama Lindsey never forgot a name or a date. She also knew when company was coming before they arrived. And when any family tragedy occurred, Mama Lindsey had already strangely been warned.

Write as soon as you can. And, as I said, we are anxiously awaiting your visit.

I had so much to tell you that I forgot the most important news. You do have a half brother, Richard Lindsey. Claude married Lois at a very early age. Richard was born before Claude went into the Air Force. However, Claude never lived with them. Lois later married Leon Blackburn, and they reared Richard (Dickie). Lois died a good many years ago. We were never around Dickie in that his mother had married again. Dickie is a schoolteacher. He taught in Muncie, Indiana, until 1974. (I did have his address there.)

In September 1974, a very tragic thing happened to Dickie. His son, William Dennis Lindsey, age 15, was stabbed and murdered in a racial incident in the school at Muncie. He was an innocent bystander. His daddy, a teacher in the school, was there and witnessed it. It was so horrible that Richard and his family moved away. I believe they live in Florida. Aunt Lura is trying to find out, and I'll send you more (and hopefully, his address) when we learn.

Richard brought his son back here for burial. Your daddy and I attended the services together. I talked briefly with Dickie and his wife, but they were so much in shock that we couldn't say much. I told him that his daddy was there, but he did not speak to Claude. He was most cordial and seemed grateful that we were there. However, I do know that Dickie, in the past years, has not had kind feelings toward Claude because of the influence of his mother.

This is all I know about Dickie. Regretfully, we were never able to know him because of the influence of Lois. But she provided a good home for him. He is a handsome and distinguished looking man. You will be very proud of him.

I'll try to close this letter again. Again, I can't begin to tell you how happy all of us are that you want to know about us and that you are planning to come.

Love,

Your cousin

Joiee

16

Dear Judi: June 22, 1977

This will be just a quick note. I'm hurrying to get ready for a quick flight to
Washington. We are tied up this time of year with TVA's budget. I'll be in one
committee meeting after another this trip. But will be back in Washington for
two weeks with the Army in September. Plan to see your daddy then, since I'll
have time over a weekend.

Hope you received my last letter in which I sent records on your great-
grandfather, Adrian Leonard Lindsey Sr., and your great-great-grandparents,
Josiah and Chealty Higgins.

Today's attachments are a continuation. But first, let me give you an address
whereby you can contact your brother Richard Lindsey:

> Mr. Richard Lindsey
> C/O Mrs. Jewel Price
> 1714 Edgehill Dr.
> Hueytown, Alabama 35020

Hueytown is almost within the city limits of Birmingham. Mrs. Price, as I think I
understand, is Richard's mother-in-law. Richard and his family have built a
home next door to Mrs. Price. They moved there after the tragedy. By the way,
you have a niece, too – Vicki (Richard's daughter).

Phillip Lindsey (attached record) is your great-great-grandfather (Adrian's
father). The location of his home place near Waterloo, Alabama, is still called
the Lindsey Place, and the creek nearby Lindsey Creek. The home burned
before my time. But I have an antique fireplace shovel that survived the fire. It
came to me by way of Caleb's heirs. (Caleb was Phillip's oldest son.)

The Lindseys settled in Cypress Inn, Tennessee (in Wayne County) about 1818 –
from Laurens County, South Carolina. They lived on Duncan Creek in that state.
Phillip had an interesting nickname – "Drummer." Of course, early salesmen
were called that, but he lived before that era of the title for salesmen---and too
he was a farmer by trade. His father, Sylvester B. Lindsey, was a captain in the
1820s in the Tennessee Volunteers (state militia). I've wondered if this may be
the source of "Drummer"--since every unit had a drummer boy. I have photo
copies of Sylvester's commissions. That of captain was signed by Sam Houston.

Incidentally, his first commission (as lieutenant) was signed by Sylvester's X mark, and his captain's commission he signed. So, he had learned to write in a matter of a few years. My theory is that the Lindseys prior to Sylvester spelled it *Lindsay*. And Sylvester's quick education resulted in the *Lindsey*. My records do not go back beyond Sylvester. However, I believe Sylvester was a son or a grandson of the Revolutionary War soldier of Wilkes County, Georgia, Major John "Silver Fist" Lindsey of the Battle of Cowpens and the Battle of Kings Mountain. A British officer cut his hand off with a saber, and he wore a silver hand – hence, "Silver Fist." Papa Lindsey always said that Dr. Carl Lindsey of Lauderdale County and Waterloo, Alabama, was his cousin. Dr. Lindsey was a descendant of Major John Lindsey. If I had the time I believe I could document our descent from Silver Fist. (I'm attaching a note on him from the historian of Maury County, Tennessee. Back to Phillip.

I have records and knew Caleb's descendants. Papa lived with them until he married after coming to Florence. I also knew Sylvester B. Lindsey II's (Phillip's son) descendants. They lived and died at Waterloo. Papa Lindsey and I used to visit Cousin Greenberry and Cousin Kern. They were delightful characters. My sister, Virginia, married into this branch of the Lindseys (descent from Sylvester II). Jackson Lindsey (Phillip's second son) was a veteran of the Civil War. He, too, was interesting. (I discovered in the old Liberty Baptist Church records that he was dismissed for drinking strong liquors.) Speaking of veterans, our Great-Grandpa Adrian (as you know already) was a four year veteran of the Confederate Army. His brother Caleb fought for the Union Army. After the war, they would not speak to one another until just before Caleb's death. Adrian was converted to Methodism not long before he died due to the powerful influence of Papa Lindsey. And mending his ways, he went at last to see his "Yankee" brother.

I could write pages on the Lindseys, but, quickly I must say a few words about the *Sharps*. This makes us kin to almost everybody in Lauderdale County. The Sharps, it seems, still own most of the land and had the most children. They were and are prosperous people – building mills, organizing banks, owning the best farms, ect. Papa Lindsey was always proud of his Sharp kin – said he was kin to every Sharp in the county – **and he was!** (I have most of the records of all the descendants in my volume of files.) Phillip Lindsey married Francis Sharp (oldest child of Charles and Matilda Anglin Sharp). The Sharps came from Virginia and settled at the Arbor near Threets Cross Roads (between Waterloo and Florence). Charles and Matilda are buried at the Arbor Cemetery. They were large landowners. Charles was a giant of a man, and there are many legends about his strength. One story I remember was that his oxen were knee-deep in a mud hole with his wagon, and Charles picked them up and set them on solid ground. An old cousin, now dead, Charles P. Sharp, swore to me this was true. (Our Adrian Lindsey was named for his uncle, Adrian Sharp.) Charles Sharp's wife was Matilda Anglin, daughter of Phillip Anglin of Patrick County, Virginia. She lived to be 113 years of age and had her teeth and did not wear glasses at her death. Our Great-Great-Great-Grandmother Matilda Sharp, lived with her daughter, Elina Jane White, during her last year. Mama Lindsey remembered her long before she met Papa Lindsey. There is a distant cousin in Mississippi writing a book on the Sharps. I don't know when he will publish it, but I will let you know. By the way, a history of Limestone County will be off the press in July ($16.05). It has two chapters about our Strange and McCuan families on Mama Lindsey's side. (I haven't sent you those records yet.) If you are interested, I will send you the address as to where you can order. Two of my friends of Limestone County wrote the book – and I supplied them with my records and some of my stories.

Judi, there is so much to tell you. I thought by sending a few records at a time I could tell you all I know. But I just keep thinking of more and more. Guess I'll have to wait until I see you (soon I hope) to finish what I can't find time and space to write.

Write when you can. I still hope you will send me a picture of Judi.

Love,
Cousin

Dear Cousin Judi: July 4, 1977

My stories of our family now arrive at the bosom of my childhood. It makes up
so much of the warmth and love all of us inherited and will treasure always.
Next to Mama and Papa Lindsey, we made our family headquarters at the big
house at the foot of the hill. Here lived the Johnsons — the parents of Mama
Lindsey. Franklin Pierce Johnson, Pappa, as he was called, was tall and lean and
wore a mustache. He was about six feet, four inches; drove the best buggy,
owned the best mare, and lived in the best house in our part of town. Pappa
was very industrious. He was superintendent in the mills, built a sizeable library
in his house, and invested in stocks, bonds, and real estate. The Johnsons,
before my time, were well-to-do people. Pappa died the year before I was born.
And by the time I can remember, the Johnsons were poor but proud and never
forgot the dignity they had once known. The old house was two-storied with a
double front porch. This porch was the gathering place of all our family,
especially late in the evening. Your daddy and all us children knew this as our
second home.

Mama Johnson (Mary Ellender McCuan Johnson) had been born in considerable
circumstances. Her father, Nelson McCuan, was a planter and raiser of fine
racehorses in Limestone County, Alabama. But he is another story to tell in
other letters to follow. (In fact, I will send you a newspaper story from
Limestone County about him that I wrote years ago.) Anyhow, the Civil War left
the McCuans destitute, Nelson was dead — and the widow moved to Florence
with her daughters to work in the mills. Mama Johnson was a daughter of
Nelson McCuan. She was a small lady (and according to your daddy, must have
looked a lot like you). Pappa Johnson would hold his arm straight out and Mama
Johnson would stand beside him and not touch his arm. She died three years
before my birth. I never knew Pappa or Mama Johnson, but they were talked of
and discussed so much by all the family that I grew up thinking I had known
them personally. They had to have been the most loved of parents because of
the esteem held for them by every child.

Aunt Maggie (Magnolia Johnson Cole) was the oldest child. In my time, she was the grand matriarch of the Johnson clan and ruled the entire household as would the Queen of England or Scotland. She was beautiful, with white wavy hair, until the day she died at the age of 88 years. I spent so many wonderful hours with her and learned all about the family for many generations. She gave me the treasured family Bible from Virginia, plus many other heirlooms that will always mean so much to me. She had a heart as big as all outdoors, and all the large family, including the great nephews and nieces, came under the special care of her wings. Aunt Maggie was a charter member of the St. James Methodist Church and taught several generations of children in the community. Everybody in this part of town loved "Miss Maggie."

I would write volumes about Aunt Maggie if only I had the time. I would tell you of her family stories and about our trips together to old family living places and cemeteries in Lauderdale, Limestone, and Colbert counties. But I must leave this noble lady now so that I can complete the story of the Johnsons.

The next child was Roscoe. He was a giant of a man, measuring six foot six in his bare feet. Uncle Roscoe never married and was murdered in Sheffield, Alabama, at the age of 34. The family never got over this tragedy, and when I was a boy, they talked of it as if it had happened only yesterday (and that was 16 years before my time). Uncle Roscoe was a railroad man, and I have many of his letters and railroad papers in my collection.

The third child was Uncle Robert McCuan Johnson, also a railroad man. He died at the age of 36 of indigestion. Today, I'm almost sure, they would say heart attack. He was a small, good-looking man and favored the McCuans. He married twice — the first time to his first cousin, Lillie Leach. He visited them in Waco, Texas, and before the family knew what was happening, they were married. They had a son, Robert McCuan Johnson Jr. Uncle Rob left Lillie and Robert Jr. and married again — this time to Clara Hendrix of Chester, Illinois, another marriage resulting from the railroad. They had a son, Roscoe Howard Johnson Jr., who died at the age of six I'll have more to say about Uncle Rob when we get to the McCuans in that Lillie was the daughter of Aunt Rebecca Ann McCuan who married first a Graham and second a Leach. The last we heard of Robert Jr., he was in California. Great-Uncle Robert Johnson is buried with our great-grandparents in the Florence Cemetery.

The fourth child was George Elliott Johnson. He, too, was a small man in size — after the McCuan side. Your uncle Marvin Lindsey looks almost exactly like Uncle Ell. Uncle Ell married Mary (Mollie) Patti of Chattanooga, Tennessee. They had no children. We visited them as long as Uncle Ell lived (he died in 1957). It was always a celebration when Uncle Ell came home — all the family would gather in for the occasion. He was full of fun, and we children loved him.

Child number five was **Lucy Lavinia Johnson**, our grandmother. (It is spelled Lucy in all the family Bibles — and she spelled it Lucy. The reason it was on Claud's birth certificate as Lucie was due to the spelling by the family doctor; he was notorious for his incorrect "ies.") I could write a library about Mama Lindsey. She was everything to all of us — love, tenderness, concern, and care. She was a historian of no second rate — remembering everything, including dates, and had a marvelous gift of weaving it all into the most exciting stories. As a child, I had the ambition to write everything down that she knew, but she didn't live long enough for me to complete the work. I have published many of her stories and have written many articles about our love as a family for her. I shall share these things with you when I can pull them from my files. As a child, I lived three doors away from Mama and Papa Lindsey. Their home was my home — and just as often as I was there, they were at our place. Your daddy, Uncle Marvin, Uncle Nelson, and Uncle Howard were more like my brothers than my own brothers — because of our closeness in years, and our closeness as a family unit. Mama Lindsey was a little woman with a **great** heart. (Your daddy says your sister Lucy looks like her and my mother, Pauline.) She was very religious, as were her sisters, her mother and father, and her husband, Papa Lindsey. I wish I had the time to write all I would love to write you about this dear soul that will always be so much a part of me.

The sixth child was Fred Johnson. He drowned in the spring branch behind the house when he was a little over a year old.

The seventh child was a girl they named Freddie in memory of her older brother. Aunt Freddie married Acy Watson, son of a Methodist preacher. They had children my age, and they were my playmates all during my growing days. The Watsons lived in a big house owned by Pappa Johnson that was next door to Aunt Maggie's. (By the way, Aunt Maggie was left a widow when she was a young 27 years of age, never remarried, and lived in the ancestral Johnson homeplace until her death.) Aunt Freddie's children were: Wylodean, Norma, Douglas, Gurley, and James.

The youngest child of Franklin Pierce and Mary Ellender (Mollie) Johnson was dear little Aunt Effie. She died only nine years ago (June 24, 1968) and was the last of a **great** family that filled such a warm place in our lives. Aunt Effie was a spinster, lived in the old homeplace with Aunt Maggie, and acted as if all of us great-nieces and nephews were her own children. She kept a ledger of all of us, and I found it not long after her funeral. It had the names of all of Claud's children, with notations of all she could learn about you. You have missed so much, Judi, by not knowing Aunt Maggie and Aunt Effie. And when I think of your coming visit, I say to myself, "How much Aunt Maggie and Aunt Effie would have welcomed you!" I have mentioned Aunt Effie in several of my feature articles. (I write feature stories, sort of a homespun nostalgic style, carried by the county newspaper.) When I have time, I will Xerox some of the ones about our family for you.

After Aunt Effie's death, the once pretentious Johnson home was torn down. One of life's sad moments was standing there watching the workers wreck the house filled with so many warm memories. I wrote one of my favorite stories about the nostalgia I felt. (I just must send you a copy of that story!)

As I think I told you, I have an ancient bedroom suit from the old Johnson place, along with Great-Great-Grandpa McCuan's beard, and other family articles that came from the rooms of this place we loved so well. These will be a part of the things I'm anxious for you and Lucy to see. I also have a lot of family photographs from the past, including all the Johnsons I have described above.

I'm attaching the family data on the Johnsons for your records. I'm also sending Pappa Johnson's brothers, sisters, mother, and father. I did not know any of these people, other than the stories told by Mama Lindsey and Aunt Maggie. But I do have pictures of all of them, except James Blassingame Johnson (Pappa Johnson's father) who died when Pappa Johnson was a small boy. Pappa Johnson's mother (Martha Nichols Johnson) lived with Pappa and Mama Johnson until her death. The Johnson home, being a large house, included a room for Grandma Johnson and Grandma McCuan. (Mama Lindsey grew up with both grandmas living in her homeplace — hence, the reason I have so much history.) I was with Aunt Maggie Johnson Cole (Mama Lindsey's sister) as she was dying, and she was talking to her Grandmother Johnson. I shall never forget her last words. "Here I am Grandma; here I am."

Martha Nichols Johnson (your great-great-grandmother) was a daughter of the Reverend William P. Nichols, early Methodist circuit rider. I'm sending you a copy of a story I wrote about him. The reason I wrote this account, Judi, which leans heavily on our Methodist heritage, is because my daughter Nancy, married Mac Buttram, a son and grandson of five generations of Methodist ministers. When my grandson, Carter Buttram, was born, his Grandfather Buttram wanted me to write this so he could include it in their family history. Hence, the Methodist trend of the story. But it gives you all I know about our great-great-great-grandpa, the Methodist preacher, William P. Nichols, and his descendants.

I will close out this volume. My next letter will be about Great-Grandma Johnson's people, the Nelson McCuans of Limestone County, Alabama. This is one of the tours I plan to take you and Lucy on — to show you the old plantation grounds and the burial places near Athens, Alabama.

Love,

Your Cousin

Judi

This Singer Sewing Machine belonged to Mary Ellender McCuan (Mammy) Johnson. It was taken from the old Johnson home on Sweetwater Avenue before the home was torn down. It is now in the home of Mildred Hanback, a

Franklin Pierce Johnson (Pappy) was a Singer Sewing Machine repairman and salesman. He is pictured here with his horse and buggy used in his work. One of his sons is shown on the buggy.

Daughters of Claude Cole, Claude was the son of Magnolia (Aunt Mag) Johnson Cole. From left: Evelyn Bennett, Mildred Hanback and Helen Blalock

August 2, 1977

Dear Cousin Judi:

Really glad to hear from you. You can guess how busy we are this week, with Suzannah's wedding coming up Thursday. Received a welcomed letter from Lucy yesterday.

Your and Lucy's visit was a highlight in our family. We have never met more charming young ladies. Your mother did an outstanding job in raising you. And no small amount of credit goes, I'm sure, to you and Lucy. We were impressed with our cousins, your culture and mannerism, your genuine warmth and love, and the southern beauty that radiates from your good looks and personality. All your kin here and about just keep talking about Judi and Lucy and how very much all of us enjoyed your visit and how much we look forward to you both coming as often as you can.

Remember the marker that was missing? Mrs. Axford (owner of the restaurant where we had lunch) found it almost immediately. The markers and graves had been moved to the old cemetery at Salem (across the road near the home of Abner's daughter, Nancy Ann Bernard). I had given TVA authorization several years ago to move the graves if and when the dam on Elk River was to be built. It seems that the owner of the field used that as his authorization. I'm far from happy about the incident, but I do feel better knowing that it was not pure vandalism. At least, ol' Abner now has a safer resting place.

And now, to continue with my words of history for your records.

This saga moves back in time to another generation, to the community of Salem in Limestone County, Alabama, and to a splendid two-story and many-roomed house that stands and is in good repair as of this writing. This was the home of our great-great-great-grandmother, Nancy Ann Mitchell Alloway Strange Bernard, and her husband, our great-great-great-grandfather, Charles M.

Bernard. (Near this house now lies the body of Abner A. Strange, as noted above.)

The Bernard home is almost two miles from Cairo, where lived our great-great grandparents, Nelson and Sarah Catherine Bernard McCuan. Sarah Catherine moved to Lauderdale County after her husband, Nelson McCuan's, death. She lived and died at the home of our great-grandparents, Franklin Pierce and Mary Ellender McCuan Johnson, and is buried in one of our ancient burial grounds — the Martin Cemetery at the Florence Golf and Country Club. This grand lady, as was her mother, was a family historian and told enchanting stories to her grandchildren, our grandmother Lindsey and her sister, our great aunt, Maggie Cole. Mama Lindsey and Aunt Maggie, in turn, passed them on to me, and I, in turn, am trying to pass on to you who have inherited the title of "family historian."

The Bernards (our great-great-great-grandparents) came to Limestone County, Alabama, in the summer of 1825 with Nancy Ann's father, Abner Alloway Strange Sr. of Fluvanna County, Virginia. At least three of his married children and their families joined the caravan. Sarah Catherine remembered her mother telling how several married daughters stayed behind in Virginia with their families. They traveled a day's journey with the group to see them off. One sad sight Nancy Ann always talked about was the final farewell to her sisters that she would never see again. They waved, she recalled, until their image finally faded into the background of the Blue Ridge Mountains of Virginia.

The trip to Alabama took about three months. Nancy Ann told about crossing the mountains and looking below to see men building the railroad bed that was to cross the Blue Ridge into the western frontier. They came by way of Tennessee, stopping to bury their dead. In that state, Abner's third wife, Mary Saunders, gave birth to the youngest of 19 children — Sarah Jane Strange, whose grave you saw at the old Lebanon Church.

Abner gave his daughter, Nancy Ann (our ancestor), the land where the stately Bernard home was built.

I do not know much about our Bernards beyond Charles M. An entry in our family Bible records the death of Elizabeth Bernard, Grandmother of Charles M., who died August 30, 1822 — only three years before the family moved to Alabama. Our great-great-grandmother, Sarah Catherine McCuan, proudly proclaimed that the Bernards were Presbyterians and were Black Dutch from Holland. While I was in Holland during World War II, I found Bernards living in Amsterdam. Our family name in Germany was spelled Bernauer. Mama Lindsey always claimed that the dark complexion beauty in her family came from the Black Dutch. And in Holland, the land of the fair skin and blond hair, it is not uncommon to see dark hair, brown eyes, and a hue in complexion to match. But I must confess to you I have, to this day, been unable to clear up the terminology "Black Dutch."

There is a community in Fluvanna County, Virginia, called "Bernardsburg." Our great-great-great-great-great-grandfather, John Alloway Strange, owned property there and referred to it in his will as "Bernerdsburg." I assume, but cannot prove, this community was named for the family of our great-great-great-grandfather, Charles M Bernard, of Fluvanna County, Virginia.

Our great-great-great-grandmother, Nancy Ann Mitchell Alloway Strange Bernard, was a remarkable lady of the Old South. And this was her full Christian name. She called herself Ann Mitchell Alloway. Her father called her Nancy Ann. She was named Ann Mitchell in honor of her mother, and the Mitchell also honored her grandmother Strange. Her mother and her paternal grandmother were both Mitchells, related by birth and marriage. The Alloway part was used by every member of the Strange family for generations. In Scotland, they were called the Alloway Branch of the Strange Clan. Ann was a historian and carefully recorded all the family data in the family Bible. This Bible had a special stand in the large entrance hall in the family home at Salem. She brought it with her all the way from Virginia. It passed through the McCuans and Johnsons to me.

When I inherited it, I took the Bible to the Archives at Nashville for inspection. The staff was so fascinated by Nancy Ann's handwriting that I was asked to allow the late Roscoe de'Armond, an expert in early penmanship, to analyze it. He said that she was a lady of noble birth and possessed an unusually good education for that era, probably in a finishing school afforded young ladies of position in early Virginia.

Nancy Ann's husband, Charles M. Bernard, died in 1827. She remained a widow until her marriage at the age of 44 to John C. Harrison in 1841, at Salem, in Limestone County. The house is sometimes called the Harrison Place today.

Incidentally, I have Ann's black bonnet that she brought from Virginia, hoping she would find a church to wear it to in the frontiers of Alabama. Her father and brother, not finding a church, were both instrumental in establishing two Methodist churches — Lebanon and Salem.

The children of Charles M. and Nancy Ann Bernard are listed on the attached chart. Great Aunt Maggie remembered how her Grandmother McCuan loved and talked about her only brother, Abner Allen Bernard. As far as I know, he did not marry and, unfortunately, the name Bernard ceased in our Clan with his early death at the age of 34.

I find it sad that someone forgot to record in our Bible the date of Nancy Ann Mitchell Alloway Strange Bernard's death. She had been so faithful to note the birth, marriage, and death of all her family during her lifetime. I figure she must have died before the Civil War and after the death of her second husband, John Harrison, because his death is noted in her handwriting. So, I place her death between 1856 and 1865. The reason I believe she was dead during the terrible Civil War is because her daughter, Great-Great Grandma McCuan, had the Bible with her when she moved to Lauderdale County, Alabama, in 1866.

The old Salem United Methodist Church, located across from Great-Great-Great Grandmother Bernard's home was built, timber and land donated by her youngest brother, Edward Saunders Strange. As I told you, the late Captain Bill Strange of Athens, who died at about 100 years of age in the 1960s, was very proud of this church and said that we Stranges were Methodist from the time of John Wesley. Before Wesley, we were of the Anglican Church (St. Peter's Parish in Virginia still carries our early baptismal records). Captain Billy Strange was a great-grandson of Abner Alloway Strange Sr. He and I made several trips together around Limestone County, and he contributed a lot to me for my collection of family lore. I pointed out the graves of Bishops and Joneses in several cemeteries while we were in Cairo and Salem. These were the families of Treana Ellender Bernard Bishop, daughter of Charles M. and Ann Bernard, and Martha Harriett Bernard Jones, daughter of Charles M. and Ann Bernard. The James H. Jones family (our Great-Great-Great-Grand-Aunt Martha) was a prosperous people. They bought her grandfather, Abner A. Strange Sr.'s place, including the rich Elk River bottomland. I knew and visited the last survivor of this family. When she died over 20 years ago, the stately old home went out of our family into other hands. Although not as well cared for now as when I used to visit there, it still is impressive, with the long double-decked front porches, stone chimneys, and stone wall in front.

Incidentally, did you notice the double-decked front porch style of each generation among the family houses we visited? This is interesting. Nelson McCuan's home (the one the Yankees burned) had the same architecture, and our great-grandparents in Florence, Franklin Pierce and Mary Ellender McCuan Johnson, carried the same style in building. This two-storied front porch lasted many generations in our family homes, from the 1820s until the 1900s.

This ends my story of our Bernards. In my next letter, we will hear more about the Stranges. However, you now have my booklet on Abner Alloway Strange, veteran of the Revolutionary War. It gives most of the family data on this line. Abner A. Strange Sr. was the father of our Nancy Ann Mitchell Alloway Strange Bernard of Virginia and Alabama.

Judi, I've been writing this over a period of a week. Since I started, we had the lovely wedding. Wish you could have been here.

I'm enclosing some pictures we made while you were here. I'm so glad I have them for my files.

Write as soon as you can. And my love to all the family.

Your cousin,

William L. McDonald
2207 Berry Avenue
Florence, Alabama 35630

November 3, 1977

Dear Cousin Judi:

The following information about our Strange family follows the booklet I gave you, ABNER ALLOWAY STRANGE SR. OF ALABAMA, SOLDIER OF THE AMERICAN REVOLUTION (by W. L. McDonald, 1955). So, at this place in your collection, you should file the booklet for continuity.

I have traced Abner's journey from Virginia to Alabama in 1824 in my letter to you with reference to his daughter and our great-great-great-grandmother, Nancy Ann Mitchell Alloway Strange Barnard. By the way, my notes are to the effect that our Virginian family originally spelled it *Barnard*. But our Alabama spelling is *Bernard*.

The Stranges were lovely people. I knew Cousin Nellie Strange Christopher well. I visited her many times and was often treated at her table with the finest cooking to be found anywhere Cousin Nellie was a first cousin to our Great-Great-Grandmother Sarah Katherine Barnard McCuan. Nellie's father was Abner's youngest son, Edmond, and Grandma McCuan's mother was Nancy Ann Mitchell Alloway Strange Bernard, who was among Abner's oldest children by his first wife. Cousin Nellie thought I favored the Stranges. She said they were all short in height, with fair hair and complexion, and the men were especially jolly and full of fun and wit. A few years ago, when Cousin Nellie died, the family invited me to preside at her funeral, and we buried her with her ancestors.

Cousin Billy Strange was another elderly member of our clan that I had a wonderful relationship with. He died in the early 1960s, at almost 100 years of age. He was known in Athens as "Cap" Strange and was probably Limestone County's wealthiest citizen at the time of his death. He was a great-grandson of Abner Alloway Strange Sr., our great-great-great-great-grandfather. Cap and I drove a lot of miles in and around Cairo and Salem as he told me about the family and showed me where they lived and were buried.

I am attaching a story and diagram of our Strange family in America from 1619 to 1824. This takes us to Fluvanna County, Virginia, where we came from in 1824.

Sadelew White, another lovely cousin, lived at Stage Junction, Virginia, in Fluvanna County. Her home was built in 1843 by her grandfather James Pleasant White on the historic Stage Road from Charlottesville to Richmond. She was born in 1843 and lived with her brother when I knew them. Cousin Sadelew was a historian, called Abner's name in such a way that one would have thought she knew him personally. She knew all our family in Virginia, as she was the family record keeper. She lived only five miles from our Oak Hill Plantation. She, too, told me that the males in our Strange family were small in height, sandy- or red-haired, and light complexioned. Cousin Sadelew was a lady of culture, quoted a lot of poems, and her favorite scripture was Joel 1:3.

Our people were landed gentry in early Virginia. We have a noble heritage.

In future letters, I shall try to carry our Strange family into Ronaldsay, Scotland, and to the year 1148.

Write soon and take care.

Love,
Your Cousin

Correction Note:

In one of my previous letters, I said that our Great-Uncle Robert McCuan Johnson, married the first time his first cousin who was a daughter of our Great-Great-Uncle Isaac Mitchell McCuan. I found in my notes a statement from

Great-Aunt Maggie that she was Lillie Leach, the daughter of our Great-Great-Aunt Rebecca Ann McCuan. Aunt Beckie married first a William Graham and second, a Mr. Leach. I do not know how I made the error in my thinking. However, change your notes to reflect who Lillie was.

August 30, 1983

Dear Judi:

I'm updating the letter I wrote to you on July 8, 1977, about the McCuans of Limestone County, Alabama. Seven years have passed since you were so interested in our family, and now you have a little family of your own. When your son is older, you will want to continue your collection, for he, too, must know his heritage.

The letters I wrote to you in those days have become collector's items for our family. I wish I had taken more time to polish them, and edit them, and proof them. They, as this, had to be dashed off in a hurry. I do hope that future generations will be kind when they find so many errors. Incidentally, these letters, collected into binders, have become known in the Lindsey family as "THE JUDI LETTERS."

Our Limestone County McCuan patriarch, Nelson McCuan, surely had to have been the most loveable character. The widow and then the daughter and then the granddaughter kept his long brownish and almost reddish beard, and Great-Aunt Maggie Cole passed it on to me to take care of in this life. My uncle, Nelson Lindsey, bears his name as well as my brother, John Nelson McDonald, and his son, John Nelson McDonald Jr. On the Starkey side, of course, there are the Nelsons — Nelson Starkey Sr. and Nelson Starkey Jr. (currently our State Representative from Lauderdale County, Alabama). They all carry the name of a man who lived more than a hundred years ago — our great-great-great-grandfather. I wrote his story, which was published in the periodical *JOURNAL OF MUSCLE SHOALS HISTORY*. I'm enclosing a copy.

Nelson's wife, Sarah Katherine, was a daughter of Nancy Ann Mitchell Alloway Strange whose husband was Charles M. Bernard. This long name is really our Great-Great-Great Grandmother Bernard's whole name. The Alloway was a part of our branch of Stranges for over two hundred years. Children — male and female — carried the Alloway in their name. The Mitchell was a family name; her grandmother and great-grandmother were Mitchells of Virginia. These stories of the Bernards, Mitchells, and Stranges will come later. This letter is about the McCuans.

As you will note in the newspaper article enclosed, two sons of Nelson and Sarah Katherine died in early years; John William was killed by lightning and Samuel died as an infant. Only one son, Isaac Mitchell McCuan, lived to be grown and indulged by five loving sisters and a mother. After Uncle Mitch moved with his mother and sisters to work in the Florence mills, he disappeared at the age of 16. As you can imagine, they thought him dead. After the lapse of 15 years, in 1885, they received a letter from him. He was living at McCrory, Arkansas. They talked about him around the family table and on the old front porch for years. In 1919, he bought a new Ford and came to see his sisters. Mitch died March 16, 1945, and was buried about two and one-half miles from McCrory, Arkansas. Here is his obituary:

I. M. McCuan funeral Sunday

Funeral services for Mr. I. M. 'Mitch' McCuan, aged 90 years, eight months and three days, were conducted at the Woodmen Cemetery, Sunday afternoon by Rev. Ralph Hillis, pastor of McCrory Methodist Church, with about 200 sorrowing friends and relatives attending.

Isaac Mitchell McCuan was born July 13, 1854, in Limestone County Alabama, and died at the home of his son, Robert L. McCuan, near McCrory, Friday, March 16, 1945, at 6:30 a.m.

Mr. McCuan came to McCrory 74 years ago at the age of 16 years and helped develop this section of Woodruff County. He was one of the oldest pioneers and devoted his entire life to farming.

He was married to Miss Lorene F. Payne on August 11, 1884, and two children from his union, Mrs. Sam Kyle of McCrory, and Marshal McCuan, of Pocatella, Idaho, survive.

After the death of their mother, Mr. McCuan spent two years in Texas and later, on November 16, 1901, married Mrs. Sallie (Thompson) Williams who preceded him in death on May 3, 1941. By this union he is survived by the following children: Robert Lee McCuan and Wilmer McCuan of McCrory, Cpl. Granville McCuan of Fort Lewis, Wash., and Pfc. Oval McCuan, of Camp Bray, Texas.

Mr. McCuan lived an honest and honorable life among us, and his word was his bond. He was well and favorably known throughout Woodruff and Cross Counties, and leaves a host of friends who mourn his loss.

Burial was in charge of Funeral Director Walter W. Raney of McCrory.

Over Labor Day weekend in 1982, I visited the McCuan Reunion in Texoma State Park, Oklahoma, and spoke about the heritage of our family back to Scotland. There I met the best people — honest, genuine, wholesome, and friendly. (I'm enclosing a copy of my article "Impressions at Texoma.") From Texoma, I came back by McCrory, Arkansas. Arriving there on Sunday at 10:50 a.m., I attended services at the McCrory United Methodist Church, and afterwards, attempted to find Uncle Mitch's folks. I found Cousin Lunnie Blanch Kyle, Uncle Mitch's daughter and only surviving child of his first marriage. Two sons are also living. Bob and Oval are of his second marriage. Blanche is over 90 years of age, lived at that time alone in a quaint little cottage on Main Street, raised flowers and a healthy garden, and, I noted, was a matchless housekeeper. Everything was as clean and orderly as was my mother's home in the old days. Imagine. Cousin Blanch is Grandma Lindsey's first cousin. I was awed to be in the presence of one from that generation yet alive. We had a delightful time. I was the first of her Aunt Mollie Johnson's folks that she had ever seen.

In the summer of 1983, I returned to McCrory for the McCuan Reunion (Uncle Mitch's descendants). There I met 101 cousins who were kind and warm people. I was welcomed into their homes and into their fellowship as one of their own.

Bob McCuan, Uncle Mitch's son, is a delight, smiling all the time. He rode to the reunion on his tractor and in overalls. He looks like every Statom — Cousin Virgil, Cousin Price, Cousin Ollie. I felt as if I had gone back in time, the resemblance was so close. Cousin Lunnie Blanche is now in a nursing home.

I shall always remember my visit and the joy of knowing Uncle Mitch's family. I do wish Mama Lindsey and Aunt Maggie could be here to share all of this with me.

Those were the brothers. Now for the daughters of Nelson McCuan.

The only one I knew — and how fortunate that my lifespan met the very last of hers — was Great-Grand-Aunt Lucy McCuan Statom. She died when I was a boy. I shall always remember being in her home, though, and her fine cooking and her immaculate house, and how proud she was. She was sick a while before her death. I recall her frail body in the high old-fashioned bed in the large log house. Then, on the day of her funeral, a terrible cloud and the torrents of rain. Aunt Lucy was the baby child. She married James Statom and they lived on a large farm out from Florence on Chisholm Highway. Their descendants live there today, and the old farm is called Statom Town. Uncle Jim had all kinds of farm animals and fowl. A gander chased me one time and caught me by the seat of the pants. Cousin Maude rescued me. What a delightful lady! She died a few years ago in the ninetieth-plus years of her life. I had a wonderful relationship with Cousin Maude and visited with her as long as she lived, even during her remaining days in the nursing home. Cousin Maude was the only daughter, but had brothers — Virgil, Chalmers, Ollie Mitchell, and Price. They all are gone now. Uncle Mitch McCuan's boys look just like them.

Great-Grand-Aunt Roseana Elizabeth McCuan, born April 7, 1850. That's all I know about her. Don't understand why. Have checked and rechecked my old notes from conversations with Mama Lindsey and Aunt Maggie. Surely, I must have gotten her mixed up with some of the things I recorded about Great-Grand-Aunt Rebecca.

Great-Grand-Aunt Rebecca Ann McCuan was the oldest child. According to my notes, she married, first, William Graham on January 16, 1863. He was a Confederate soldier at the time. They had children and moved to Allsboro, Alabama, in Colbert County. Aunt Maggie said they were very poor and lived under hard circumstances. Later, I pick them up in my notes at Waco, Texas. Her second marriage was to a Leach and they had more children, including Lillie, a good-looking daughter. Our Great-Uncle Robert Mitchell McCuan (Mama Lindsey's brother) worked with the railroad, visited Aunt Kan (that's her family name taken from Beckie Ann), and married Lillie, his first cousin. They had one son, Robert Mitchell McCuan Jr. Uncle Rob left Lillie and Robert Jr. and later married Clara Hendrix. They had one son, Roscoe Howard, who died in 1917.

Anyhow, back to Lillie. I have letters in my file from Lillie begging Robert to come back. Really sad, but we do not know all the circumstances. We never heard from Robert Jr. Judge Simpson of Florence was traveling out west in the 1930s and said he stopped at a service station in California but couldn't remember the town. The owner of the station noticed the Alabama tag and told him that he was Robert Johnson Jr. and that he had several aunts living in Florence. That's all we ever knew about Rob's son, Robert Jr. Now, back to Aunt Kan. When Uncle Mitch McCuan's first wife died, he left Arkansas and went to live with his oldest sister, Aunt Kan. Cousin Lunnie Blanche (Uncle Mitch McCuan's daughter in McCrory, Arkansas) said that Aunt Kan was living with a retarded son on a farm and her father, Uncle Mitch, tended the farm for a couple of years until they (Uncle Mitch and family) moved back to McCrory, Arkansas, to the 280-acre farm they had inherited from Uncle Mitch's first wife's father.

Great-Grand-Aunt Martha Harriet McCuan married William L. Toon, a Confederate soldier. She had two daughters, Willie and Mary Elizabeth. Willie died young and is buried at the Florence Golf and Country Club beside her grandmother, our Great-Great-Grandmother McCuan. Mary Elizabeth married Newton Starkey of Limestone County and lived for many years on the farm once owned by her father, Nelson McCuan. Her house was still standing when I was there last summer.

When my mother was a little girl (along about 1914 or 1915, I guess), a drummer came by Great-Grandma Johnson's home selling goods. As was the custom in those days, he was invited to eat with them. In the conversation, he mentioned coming by way of Limestone County. Great-Grandma told him that she had a sister at Cairo, and they had lost contact with her for more than 40 years. He had been to Aunt Pattie's (that's Great-Grand-Aunt Martha Harriett McCuan Toon) and told them exactly how and where to find her. A large caravan was organized with all the Johnsons and Statoms. It took two days to make the long trip. They camped for the first night on Bluewater Creek. What a sight as they came across the hill into Cairo! Aunt Pattie was at church; there was a summer revival going on. Cousin Nelson Starkey was a small boy and he ran to hide in the barn, thinking it was a Gypsy caravan. His brother, Carlos, was sent to fetch Aunt Pattie from church, telling her that her two lost sisters and their families were at the Starkey home. She came across the hill shouting and crying! What a story! The Starkeys and Johnsons talked about that event as long as they lived. Every time I visit Nelson, he likes to tell again the saga of the buggies and wagons that appeared one day in Cairo!

We have always been close to the Starkeys. Nelson Sr. and his wife, Bessie, ran a boarding house and Starkey's Restaurant in Florence for many years.

Nelson McCuan's father was Isaac McCuan of the Shenandoah Valley of Virginia. In my article, I said it was Petersburg, Virginia. Our cousin from Texas, Noble McCuan, called my hand, and sure enough, I was wrong. I rechecked my notes, and it was Papa Lindsey's Sharps who hailed from Petersburg. Our McCuans came from the lovely Shenandoah. In Virginia and other parts of America, they spelled it McCune. Limestone County, Alabama, is the exact origin of the spelling "McCuan." In Scotland, they were MacEwans. So, the Americanization of the MacEwans is an interesting study that leads to our lovely state of Alabama.

When Nelson McCuan died at the end of the terrible Civil War (and he had lost so much and had been so mistreated), his father came, according to our family stories, all the way from Virginia in a nice buggy and begged Nelson's widow, Sarah Katherine, to return to Virginia with him. She wouldn't, and Mama Johnson would express wonder. She said her Grandfather Isaac was wealthy, and they wouldn't have had such a hard time if her mama had gone with Grandpa back to Virginia.

Instead, Sarah Katherine McCuan moved to Florence, Alabama, with her daughters and one son and worked in the Globe Cotton Mill. What a sad decision. She left her farm in Cairo and it later became the property of others by right of her abandoning it and their paying the taxes. When I first went to Cairo, the owners of the properties were somewhat suspicious of my being there. They thought I had come back to give them trouble. So, I guess their deeds are still not all that clear in title.

I could go on and on about the McCuans. I have so many notes about them. And I feel that I know more about them because of Mama Lindsey and Aunt Maggie. The McCuans made up most of their old stories on the front porch in the long ago. But, I must bring this to a close. Next time, I will carry you back into the Bernards, Stranges, and Mitchells and to the Orkney Islands of Scotland.

Your Cousin,

William Lindsey McDonald

41

September 9, 1983

Dear Judi:

This is another rewrite; this time, to correct and update some family information. This letter should replace the one I wrote to you on June 22, 1977.

Philip Lindsey was your great-great-grandfather. He was Adrian's father. The location of his home place is near Threet's Crossroads in Lauderdale County on Lindsey Creek. Here was his gristmill, flourmill, and home. In fact, part of the old structure, as far as I know, is still standing. I have an antique shovel that once served the big fireplace given to me by descendants of his son, Caleb Lindsey. Philip was known by the name "Drummer" Lindsey. He probably got that title by either selling his products from his mills or by being a drummer for the militia explained below.

Philip's father was John Lindsey who was born around 1765 and settled early in Cypress Inn, Tennessee. This is in Wayne County and is almost on the Alabama line. The Lindseys came from South Carolina. Dr. Carl Lindsey, born 1873, and son of Alonzo Lindsey (born 1841) and Etha Hagan (daughter of John H. Hagan and Mary Bumpass) claimed to be descended from John Lindsey of the Revolutionary War. This John served as a major in the South Carolina militia and lost his hand by a saber cut. A silver knob was fitted to the stump and he was forever afterwards called "Silver Fist" Lindsey. If Dr. Eugene Carl Lindsey was thus descended from "Silver Fist," so, I think, are we. However, I have not been able to tie our John (born about 1765) with John "Silver Fist." I'm still looking. Speaking about Dr. Lindsey, as I noted, his father was Alonzo Lindsey. Almost every generation for years carried this name. Our Grandpa Lindsey had a first cousin, Alonzo, who worked in the old Florence Wagon Factory. I remember him well.

I know that every family researcher has a story or two about two brothers, three brothers, or such that came to America. One went west, the other east, and so

42

forth. We have the same kind of tradition. Maybe such has happened over and over, but we need, also, to remember that a hundred more of the same name could have arrived on the next 10 ships. Be that as it may, our family story relates that in 1744, five brothers, John, Amos, William, Robert, and Ezekial Lindsey came to America from Dumfrieskirk, Scotland. Most of them were in South Carolina. Our folks, as related above, came to Wayne County, Tennessee, and overflowed the Alabama line to fill up Waterloo, Wright, and parts of Florence.

We have two old documents that were found in Caleb Lindsey's trunk after his death. (Caleb was Philip's son.) These were military commissions for the Wayne County, Tennessee, militia made out to Sylvester B. Lindsey. One as a second lieutenant signed by the first governor of Tennessee, and the other as a captain signed by none other than the famous Sam Houston, then governor of Tennessee. Now, I assumed until recently that since these were among the collection of Caleb Lindsey that Sylvester must surely have been his grandfather — i.e., Philip's father. Not so I have learned. Philip's father was John Lindsey (c. see article 'Soldier Boy in Blue' about John L. Lindsey, 1765) and Sylvester B. and Philip were both sons of John. Now, let it be known that Philip Lindsey named one of his boys Sylvester B., which was a custom in those days to name children after their uncles as well as their fathers and grandfathers. For the sake of clarity, I refer to Philip's son, Sylvester B., as Sylvester B. II. He was known as "Sil" Lindsey. I knew his grandson, Greenberry Lindsey, and most of my Lindsey data came from my visits with him. His father was also Greenberry, and there are lots of old family stories about the two Greenberrys. Papa Lindsey and I would visit Greenberry Jr. since Papa was cousin not only to him but his wife also (she was a Sharp).

I referred to Philip Lindsey as being called by the name "Drummer." One of my theories is that since his brother Sylvester was captain of the local militia, and Philip was a younger brother, Philip could have been the boy drummer. It's a colorful thought, anyway. Incidentally, when Sylvester B. signed his first commission, he had to make an X mark. When he signed his captain's commission, he had by then learned to write and signed it as *Lindsey*. On the first commission, even though he had an X, it was made out to Sylvester B. *Lindsay*. I don't know whether this is significant or not.

As were most Lauderdale County families, the Lindseys were divided between the North and the South during the tragic Civil War. Philip's son Caleb fought for the North and our great-granddaddy never forgave him. Greenberry told me that one time when Adrian came home on leave, Caleb saw him coming and headed for the hills...forgetting his hat. When Grandpa Adrian saw the Yankee hat, he headed after his brother, but fortunately, never caught him. After the war, they never spoke. Another of Philip's sons was Jackson Lindsey of Threet's Crossroads. He fought for the Confederacy. I noticed in the records of the Liberty Baptist Church at Threet's Crossroads that they put Uncle Jackson out of the congregation due to his drinking.

Our great-grandpa was Adrian (another of Philip's sons). He fought four years for the Confederacy in the 27th Alabama Infantry Regiment. He was crippled during the Baton Rouge Battle and limped for the remainder of his life. During his last days, he lived with our Grandpa Lindsey, and my mother said when they would run through the house, old Ade would beat his cane on the floor and yell, "The damn Yankees are here!" By the way, Ade married the second time to Belle Culver, the grandmother of Lauderdale County's richest industrialist, E. L. Culver. As long as Papa Lindsey lived, Culver and his wife, Edith, would visit with Papa and traded with him while Papa was in the grocery business. We have a painting of Great-Grandpa Adrian "Aid" Lindsey in his Confederate uniform hanging at the top of the stairwell. He was a tough-looking old solider. Before he died, he was converted and joined the Methodist Church. Papa would often quote the scripture that changed his life. For the life of me, I can't now remember what it was, but it was from the Old Testament. When Great-Grandpa Adrian Leonard Lindsey Sr. died, they placed him in Soldier's Rest at the Florence Cemetery. Several years ago, I worked with Ellen B. Henley and we restored that historic site. Grandpa's gravestone is the first one you see when you approach the area.

Our Grandpa Lindsey was mighty proud of his Sharp kin. He claimed that every Sharp in these parts was related. His grandpa, Philip Lindsey, married Frances Sharp. The Sharps came from Virginia and settled at the Arbor near Threet's Crossroads. Charles and Matilda Anglin Sharp are buried at the Arbor Cemetery, which now lies behind Junior Lovelace's barn. Charles Sharp, they say, was a giant of a man, and there are legends today about his super strength.

One of our distant cousins, Charles Sharp, namesake of the original, told me several years ago about an ox stuck knee deep in the mud along with the wagon. Our Great-Great-Great-Grandpa Charles Sharp picked them up — ox and wagon — and put them on solid ground.

Charles's wife was Matilda Anglin, daughter of Phillip Anglin of Patrick County, Virginia. Our Great-Great-Great-Grandma Matilda lived to be 113 years of age, had her teeth, and did not wear glasses at her death. In her last years, she lived with her daughter, Eliza Jane White (and I have her picture in my folder). Our Grandma Lindsey remembered Matilda in her lifetime.

This catches us up to date on the Lindseys and Sharps. At least, it is most of the important things I can remember at this time about some mighty wonderful people.

Your cousin

September 13, 1983

Dear Cousin Judi:

It's a wonderful day. We knew about you, and now we are becoming acquainted with Uncle Claude's family.

There are so many things you need to know about us.

How unfortunate that you missed Mama and Papa Lindsey, our grandparents. They've been gone for a good many years now, but let me tell you about them.

Mama Lindsey was Lucy Lavania Johnson, daughter of Franklin Pierce and Mary Ellender McCuan Johnson. Mammy Lindsey was quite small in height. Her young pictures show that she was a real beauty. She always wondered why Papa picked her; she was too young, she thought, and all the older girls were after him. Papa knew a thing or two! Mama was in every way a grandmother. She looked like one, talked like one, and loved all of us just like a grandmother in a book is supposed to do. But Mama Lindsey's love was more real and far more unique than any author could possibly have captured in a book. She loved her family, talked a lot about the old days, and could hold one spellbound with her details about dates and her sagas about history. In fact, my love for writing and my interest in history stems, I think, from all the times on the old front porch when I developed the notion to write down all of Mama's stories so that they could never become lost or forgotten.

Mama was religious and grew up in the Methodist Church. That's all she knew as far as modes of faith, yet she was a learned Bible scholar. She had a scripture for every occasion. What a delightful and wonderful person our Grandmother Lindsey was! She kept a clean house, always with a refreshing aroma. In the springtime, flowers were placed about every room. Her yard was a garden with ground ivy, sweet shrubs, and buttercups. Her favorite was a seven bark that she had carefully uprooted from her childhood home and tended through the years near the front gate. Mama had a sixth sense. She always knew when company was coming or when someone was sick or was dying. We loved her dearly. She suffered several months before her death. I was in the Army at Fayetteville, North Carolina. Uncle Howard was there, too. We came home by way of Camp McCall where we picked up Cousin Raymond Glenn. Mama Lindsey lived a few days after we got home. Dorothy sat up with her the night she died. I could write volumes about the little Southern Grandma who lived on our old hill and gave me my Christian names — William and Lindsey.

Mama is buried beside her mother, father, and brothers in the old Florence Cemetery. When Papa died, we placed him beside her. Aunt Maggie told me not long after Papa's death that they both were in Heaven; she dreamed they were walking together across a field of lovely flowers.

Papa Lindsey was born in 1878, during the worst of the Reconstruction. He was the youngest child of Adrian Leonard Lindsey Sr. and his wife, Martha Higgins Lindsey. Adrian, or "Aid," was a Confederate veteran and had come home to find all that he had ever owned gone. His wife Martha was a half Chickasaw Indian; her mother, Chealty, was born on Koger Island in the Tennessee River in 1813. When Papa Lindsey was eight years old, his mother died and Adrian married again to Mrs. Belle Culver who had children of her own. She and Aid had a daughter, Papa's half sister who, the last we knew, was living somewhere up north. Papa's stepmother was cruel to him and he talked about it a lot. I remember one story well. He would plow all day and come in late in the evening, hoping just maybe he could find a warm meal at the table. As Papa entered the barn to put up the mules, he would look up at the rafter, and there would be his supper — cold peas and cornbread.

Dr. Sullivan at Waterloo tried to adopt Papa, but Adrian would never consent. The doctor said that he would give him the very best education. Papa always said that if Dr. Sullivan had adopted him, he could have been a preacher.

Adrian Leonard Lindsey Jr. — If Papa knew the Adrian was on his name, we never knew. I didn't learn until after his death when I found it among his dad's pension records in Montgomery. Papa called himself L. Lindsey. That was what appeared on the front of his store building and on the delivery truck. His cousins and friends at the place of his birth called him Len. He was officially registered as a voter as Leonard Lindsey.

He was born in a saddlebag house in Wright, Alabama. It's gone now, but Papa took me there many times. Later, the family moved up on Manbone Creek near Waterloo. It seems that Papa's earliest impressions of his mother were at that place. He liked to visit a rock on the creek where she washed her clothes. I can see him standing there now with tears in his eyes. She represented the only love he knew in his early formative years.

Papa and one of Mose Wright's boys went to Texas when Papa was about 16 or 17. Mr. Wright used to laugh with Papa about it, but Papa didn't laugh. He said Texas was so wicked, he came home. Then was when he appeared in Florence and was staying with his Uncle Caleb's family. He had found work in the Florence Wagon Factory. Papa joined the Baptists, but after he married Mama Lindsey, he became a Methodist. And that became the **greatest** event of his life. He was one of the most loyal Methodists I have ever known. When we placed him in the nursing home at Russellville in his last days, he made it down to the Russellville First Methodist and joined. I asked him why he moved his membership from where it had been for 60 years. He looked at me with surprise and said, "Son, I'm a Methodist, and we Methodists move our membership to where we live." He did the same thing with his registration to vote, and when he died, he was a registered voter in the town of Russellville, Alabama.

I never knew why Papa took a special liking to me. We became the closest of friends until the day he went away. He would take me to church with him and make me sit on the second seat from the front. That was always his seat. After I married, Dorothy and I came to church and sat near the back. Papa looked around and spotted me. He got up and came back and led Dorothy and me to where he thought we ought to be. To this day, I think I would feel mighty uncomfortable sitting anywhere but near the front in any church.

Some folk thought Papa was strange. He was different. Lacking real love during his early boyhood years, I think it was not easy for him to show affection. Yet, he had a heart of gold. Some said that Mr. Lindsey was as stingy as a Scotsman. One time, we went together to visit his former teacher, Miss Mary Houston. She was nearing 100 years and living in dire need. Papa gave her every dollar he had in his billfold. I've seen him do other deeds just as touching.

Papa walked as straight as an Indian, had ways like an Indian and was, of course, a quarter Indian. He always dressed immaculately, wore a tie every day of the week and a coat every month of the year. When he went into the nursing home, he placed his shoes outside his door to be polished. Of course, the nursing home didn't provide such services, but the head nurse told me that his shoes were so well groomed that he didn't know the difference. Papa was first and foremost a gentleman.

He died on Memorial Day in 1960. One of his nurses looked out early to check on him and he was working in the garden. She said he was softly singing "Are You Washed in the Blood of the Lamb." Later, when she checked on him, he was lying among the roses. He lived a few days. At the last, I was holding his hands and commented that his hands were cold. Surprised at my lack of knowledge, he said, "Why, sure they are; I'm dying, you know."

Papa had a tremendous influence in my life. I shall never forget visiting my grandson, Carter, at Haleyville. He reached out for me, and I saw Papa's expression in his eyes. I knew then that a long grandfather-to-grandson relationship was beginning all over again.

There is no stopping place in the stories I would like to tell about Mama and Papa Lindsey. Yet, I must someway close this letter. In future letters, I plan to tell you what I know about each generation. Mama Lindsey's family came from

Virginia. Her Stranges settled near Jamestown in 1619 from the Orkney Islands off the northern coast of Scotland. My records of her people go back to 1148 A.D., although in some cases, between 1148 and 1500, I have names of grandfather to grandson (with the father link missing) due to the passing of land titles.

I have the family Bible brought to Alabama in 1824 from Virginia, with the first entry in 1761 as well as Great-Great-Great-Grandmother's bonnet she brought along in the covered wagon hoping there would be a church in the wilderness so that she could wear it. Among other things, I also have Great-Great-Grandpa McCuan's beard that Aunt Maggie extracted a promise from me that I would always take care of — much to my wife's and daughter's dismay. I also have the Johnson bed, which belonged to our family even before their generation.

I hope to hear from you and, better still, to visit with you.

And, you shall hear more soon — about the Lindseys, Johnsons, McCuans, and all the other branches and limbs in our family heritage.

Your cousin,

William Lindsey McDonald

Appendix 1 – Strange – McCuan

Abner A. Strange Sr.

Of Alabama

Solider of the American Revolution

F orence, Alabama

1955

ABNER ALLOWAY STRANGE

REVOLUTIONARY WAR SOLDIER OF ALABAMA

By William Lindsey McDonald, Florence, Alabama, October 1964

Abner Alloway Strange, soldier of the American Revolution under General Marquis de Lafayette[1], is buried in the middle of an Alabama cotton field near Athens in Limestone County on the bank of Elk River.

He was born March 17, 1761,[2] to a Virginian planter — John Alloway Strange[3] and his wife Ann Mildred Mitchell. John was a descendant of the Alloway branch of the Scottish Stranges. For many generations, this family used Alloway in the name of every child, whether male or female. It derives from the early home of the father of Robert Burns, the Scottish poet, near Ayr.[4]

Two brothers, William and Robert, were the first of the Alloway Stranges to settle in America. William, who was Abner's ancestor, landed at Jamestown, Virginia, on the ship *George* in 1619 and resided at "Fluerdeon Hundred" until 1623. He then returned to Scotland and married a highland wife. In 1635, this young family, now with son, Edmond Alloway, sailed to America on Captain Leonard Bett's ship *Pauline*. They landed in Virginia in July of 1635 where

51

William received a grant of 1,290 acres near Jamestown "extending into the woods."[5]

Their son, Edmond, lived and left descendants in Fluvanna County, Virginia. Robert Strange, who joined his brother William and family on the ship *Pauline* lived and left descendants in Kent County, Virginia.

The Stranges came from South Ronaldsky, Scotland. Earliest records of this family date back to the twelfth century to Kirkwall on the Island of Pomona in the Orkneys of Scotland.[4]

Abner's father, John Alloway Strange, possessed several large tracts of land in Fluvanna County, Virginia, according to his will dated June 7, 1810.[6] Abner, in his will dated July 29, 1834[7], bequeathed his part of his father's estate to be equally divided among all his children.

Abner Alloway Strange first joined the Continental Army in the fall of about 1779 as a substitute for Mile Caney of Albemarle County, Virginia. He served three months during this enlistment at Williamsburg, Virginia, in the regiment commanded by Colonel William Cabel. After this service, he was "drafted" in his own behalf[1] and served under a Captain Thompson. They marched through Petersburg to Bobbin Point on the James River and up and down the James River to repel a threatened invasion of the British.[1]

During his third period of service, Strange served as a guard under Captain Richard Wappier at the Albemarle Barracks. Here, he guarded the English prisoners captured when Lieutenant General John Burgoyne surrendered at Saratoga.

Sergeant Strange's[8] fourth and final period of service was during the 1781 campaign that led to Cornwallis' surrender at Yorktown in October of that year. At this time, Abner was with General Lafayette. His immediate commanding officer was Captain Anthony Kaden. Sergeant Strange noted that he "recollects to have seen and known Lafayette, General Wayne, Colonel Richardson, Major Campbell, and Major Armstrong."[1]

In 1781, Abner married Elizabeth A. She died January 27, 1803,[9] leaving him with ten children. They were: Gideon M., Judith A., Abner A. Jr., Ellenoir, Mildred A., Thomas M. A., John, Rebecca, Martha H. A., and Ann Mitchell Alloway.

On December 10, 1805, Abner married Mary Saunders. He was 44 years of age and she was 24. They had nine children — Harriet Vanison, Elizabeth Mitchell, Jamima Vanison, Archiles Michel[-0], George, Edward Saunders, Sarah Jane, and two others whose names are not legible on the aged Bible records.

It was in June of 1825 that Abner Strange, then 64 years old, gathered his family and possessions and moved to Alabama. They crossed the mountains into Tennessee where Mary delivered her youngest child, Sarah Jane.

At least three of Abner's married children by his first wife attached their covered wagons to the Alabama-bound caravan. They were Abner Alloway Jr., Nancy Ann Mitchell Alloway Bernard, and Martha A. Flanagan.

It was a tragic trip for Abner Jr. and his family. His wife Sallie died on the journey and two children, John Gideon and Lucy Ann, died a few weeks after reaching their new home. Abner Jr.'s other children who made the trip were: Elizabeth A., Joab A., Reuben A., Thomas A., and Abner A. III. Abner A. Strange Jr. died at the end of his first year in Alabama.[9]

Nancy Ann Mitchell Alloway Strange Bernard made the long journey with her husband, Charles M. Bernard, and four children: Abner Allen, Mary Elizabeth, Treana Ellender, and Ann Mitchell. Mary Elizabeth died in about a year after they reached Alabama. The Bernards had two more children born in Alabama — Martha Harriet and Sarah Catherine.

Martha A. Strange Flanagan and her husband, Simpson B. Flanagan, brought along at least one child on the trip — John M. Flanagan. Another child, Abner, was born during their second year in Alabama. This family left many descendants around Athens, Alabama.

Old Abner and his many descendants settled on the banks of Elk River where he acquired several large tracts of fertile land. The house that Abner built of yellow poplar logs stood for 136 years — and was still solid when it was torn down in 1961.[12]

The veteran of the War for American Independence died August 27, 1835.[13] His wife Mary lived until April 13, 1870.[14] Their graves overlook the site that was once their home near the Buck Island Bridge over Elk River. A white marble Revolutionary marker[15] now stands as a sentinel to mark one of the few known graves of Revolutionary War soldiers buried in Limestone County, Alabama.

THE FAMILY OF JOHN ALLOWAY STRANGE OF FLUVANNA COUNTY, VIRGINIA

Earliest census records of Fluvanna County show the John A. Strange family consisted of six whites and eleven slaves.

The known children of John Alloway and Ann Mildred Mitchell Strange were:

1. Patty, born September 22, 1756 (baptized October 31, 1756)

2. Abraham[16], who married Mary Moore. They had at least two children:

Archeleous, born July 12, 1780 (baptized October 21, 1781)

George Walker, born September 27, 1781 (baptized October 21, 1781)

3. Abner Alloway, born March 14, 1761 (baptized May 6, 1761)

4. Gideon A. Strange[17] His children were:

Ann Mildred (married a Carrington in 1840)

James M. (married Harriet P. Mayo)

Sallie Willie

Elizabeth

Hattie M. (married T. H. Tutwiler of Alabama)

The following excerpts from the will of John A. Strange[18] show the division of his Fluvanna County property. He appointed his son Abner A. Strange as one of the executors of the will.

> "...It is my will and desire that my wife Mildred should reside on, hold, possess, and enjoy six hundred acres of my tract of land whereon I now live to be laid off at the south side of the said tract so as to include the plantation dwelling house and other houses and the mills during her life or widowhood, and it is my will and desire that the said land and appurtenances after her decease or intermarriage be the property of my son Gideon A. Strange..."

> "...Thirdly, I give to my grandson Jessie A. Strange son of my son John A. Strange, my house and lott in the town of Barnerdsburg whereon there is a tan yard..."

> "...As to the rest of my estate both real and personal I make no will respecting the same but leave it subject to the operation of law in its divisions distribution as tho' I had died intestate..."

TO AMERICA

By William Lindsey McDonald

William Strange, born in 1601, crossed over to England from his native Scotland and enlisted in the Royal Navy at the early age of 18. He was sent on a special mission to the American shores on the ship *George*. William landed near Jamestown, Virginia, in the latter part of 1619. In 1623, his name is listed as a resident of Fluerdeen Hundred, a little distance from Jamestown.

Being a resident in the American Virginian Colony before the Pilgrims landed at Plymouth Rock, William returned to England soon after 1623, and then home to his native Scotland. Here, in a course of time, he took to himself a highland wife. Soon a son was born, Edmond Alloway Strange.

In the year 1635, the British Navy entrusted William and his brother, Robert, with another mission to America for the crown. This trip was made on the ship *Pauline* under the command of Leonard Betts. William brought with him his wife and five-year-old son, Edmond Alloway Strange. They landed in Virginia during the month of July in the year 1635.

The old passenger lists of the London Port shows the following:

> PASSINGER WCH PASSED FROM YE PORT OF LONDON
>
> XJ⁰ JULY 1635
>
> In the Paule of Lond Leonard Betts Mr bound to Virginea P Certificate from the Minister of Gravesend of their Comfortie to the Church of England.
>
> ....
>
> Wm Strange .... age 25.

Edmond Alloway Strange, son of William, the first of the American Stranges, lived and left descendants in Fluvanna County, Virginia. His uncle Robert lived and left children in Kent County, Virginia. The Alabama Stranges are descended from Edmond of Fluvanna County through Abner Alloway, who came from Virginia in 1824.

The following record from the Abstracts of Virginia Land Patents shows a grant of 1,290 acres near Jamestown to William Strange and associates for service, November 26, 1635:

(291) William Barker, mariner, Richard Quoyning and John Sadler, merchants, and their associates and company, 1,290 acres in the county of Charles City, and extending into the woods from a seat called Merchants Hope, formerly granted to the said Wm Baker, his associates an company. Due for the transportation of 20 persons (name below) Granted by West, November 26, 1635.   Georg Gregory, Thos Peacock, Wm Rodway, Jane Rodway, <u>Wm Strange</u>, Jon Yates, Jon Minter, Dorothy Standish, Matthew Robinson, Daniel Godwin, Jon Jones, Thos Johnson, George Brooks, Sarah Cullybrant, Elizabeth Phillips, Jon Crost, Daniel Bromley, Wm Woodgate, Alex Goodwin, Robert Yates, Wm Griffin, Wm Andrews, Benjamin Ragg, Wm Jackson, Nathaniel Deane.

OUR BERNARD FAMILY

This part of our saga continues in Limestone County, Alabama. However, we go this time to the Salem Community, which is not far from the home of Nelson McCuan in the Cairo Community.

Nelson McCuan's wife, Sarah Catherine, was a Bernard, and her father and mother were Charles Mitchell Bernard and Ann Mitchell Alloway Strange

Bernard. They were first cousins as well as man and wife. They married February 1, 1812, at Fluvanna County, Virginia.

I have their Bible, which was published in 1811. The earliest entries are in Great-Great-Great-Grandmother Ann Bernard's handwriting. A number of years ago, I had the staff at the State Archives in Nashville look at it. They were fascinated by her penmanship. One of the staff said it indicated that she was a lady of noble birth and possessed an unusually good education for that era, probably in a finishing school afforded young ladies of position in early Virginia. This Bible passed to my great-great-grandmother, Sarah Catherine Bernard McCuan, upon the death of her mother, Ann. Sarah Catherine brought it with her when she moved to Florence and left it with her daughter, Mary Ellender McCuan Johnson, my great-grandmother. She passed it to her eldest daughter, Magnolia Johnson Cole, who presented it to me about a month before her death.

Charles and Ann Bernard moved in the family caravan to Limestone County, Alabama, in the summer of 1825, along with her father, Abner Alloway Strange Sr., his third wife, and younger members of the family. There were also other married brothers and sisters who made this trip. Many interesting stories have been told about this long journey. The family members who were left behind in Virginia, for instance, followed them all the way to the mountains and waved goodbye, as far as they could see them, as they vanished into the wilderness. Stories, too, were passed on that tell of the railroad being cut through the mountains as our family passed by.

Charles Mitchell Bernard died July 15, 1827, only two years following their move to Alabama. Ann remained a widow until she was 44 years of age. Her second marriage was to John C. Harrison in 1841 at Salem in Limestone County. Their home, sometimes called the Harrison Place, stands today near the Salem Methodist Church.

I have Ann's black bonnet that she brought from Virginia hoping she would find a church to wear it to in the frontiers of Alabama. Her husband, Charles, along with her father, Abner, and brothers, were instrumental in establishing two Methodist churches — Lebanon and Salem. As stated earlier, our families have been Methodists for almost as long as there has been a church of this faith. Charles Bernard's three brothers — Allen Rodney Bernard, Overton Bernard, and Joab Bernard — were early Methodist preachers who played important roles in the history of American Methodism in Virginia. According to some of the stories told by Sarah Catherine Bernard McCuan to my grandmother Lucy Johnson Lindsey, one of her uncles became president of a college and wrote a number of books. He was a well-known educator of his time.

This great-great-grandmother, Sarah Catherine Bernard McCuan, moved to Florence after the death of her husband Nelson McCuan. This was in 1866, following the terrible Civil War that left her destitute. Her neighbors advised her to move to Florence and to put her children at work in the cotton factories. It was bad advice. Nonetheless, she did just that.

In her elderly years, Sarah Catherine lived with two of her daughters, alternating first with our Great-Grandmother Mary Ellender McCuan Johnson, and next with our Great-Great-Aunt Lucy Frances McCuan Statom. Thus, while living with our Johnson family, she related story after story about her people to my grandmother, Lucy Lavania Johnson Lindsey.

She told about her folks in Virginia being large landowners and was always quick to say that her family were Methodists all the way back to the time of John Wesley and that three of her uncles were Methodist preachers. Her grandfather, she would say, was a Representative from Fluvanna in the legislature at Richmond and that he, too, was a business owner at Richmond as well as in another Virginia county. These stories, along with many others that she told, I have been able to verify. She would say, too, that her family was Black Dutch. I'm still working on this. However, currently, I can only guess that at some early date, our Bernards probably migrated from Holland to England. This would have had to have been before 1700, because I found our ancestor, John Bernard Sr., in England in 1700.

Great-Great-Grandmother Sarah Catherine was Bernard McCuan's mother. The lovely name Nancy, as you know, is a diminutive of the name Ann. Therefore, she was known by Nancy. This is noted in her father's will. He referred to her as Nancy.

I will cover her father, Abner Alloway Strange, later. My records of the Strange family go back to the 11th century in Scotland.

This part of my saga covers the family of Charles Mitchell Bernard and goes back to about 1450 A.D. in England.

As I have already mentioned, Charles Mitchell Bernard and his wife, Ann Mitchell Alloway Strange, were first cousins. Charles' mother, Ann Mitchell Bernard, and Ann's mother, Elizabeth A. Mitchell Strange, were sisters. Their father was Thomas Mitchell III of New Kent County, Virginia. In fact, Ann Mitchell Alloway Strange Bernard's grandmother, Ann Mitchell (wife of John Alloway Strange), was sister to Thomas Mitchell III. Therefore, we are directly descended from our common ancestors, Thomas Mitchell Jr. and his wife Elizabeth, three ways — through the Bernards and Stranges. No wonder so many of our people carry Mitchell as either their first or middle names, even to the present generation.

Before I get away from the Bernards, our great-great-great-great grandfather, Allen Bernard (born January 29, 1743; died July 4, 1834), was a popular physician in Fluvanna County, Virginia. He also held a commission as major in the Second Battalion, Twelfth Virginia Regiment, and from 1796 to 1805, and served as a Representative in the Virginia House of Delegates. The town of Bernardsburg in Fluvanna County, Virginia, was created in 1796 on his plantation. All of these interesting things about him were related by Great-Great Grandmother Sarah Catherine to my Grandmother Lucy; and in recent years, they, too, have been confirmed by records that I have seen.

The attached charts show interesting information about the Bernards and go back to 1700 in England. They have information about the children and their marriages. This would take pages and pages of narration here; so, I refer you to the attached family record charts.

Note that we are directly descended from the following families: Bernard, Mitchell, Moss, Barnett, Farrar, Perrin, Banks, Royall, Abney, Lacy, and Strange. All of these are covered, generation by generation, in the attached family charts — some going all the way back to the 11th century. However, I plan to write more in this narration about our Great-Great-Great-Great-Grandfather Abner Alloway Strange Sr., at or near the end of this document. He was a Revolutionary War veteran. I have a considerable amount of family information that I have collected about him and his ancestors that I'm sure you would like to know.

OUR STRANGE FAMILY

This continues our family saga. Our great-great-great-grandmother, Ann Mitchell Alloway Strange Bernard (she was called "Nancy" by her family), was daughter of Abner Alloway Strange Sr. and Elizabeth Ann Mitchell. As I've already mentioned, Ann and Charles were first cousins as well as man and wife.

Abner Alloway Strange was a veteran of the American Revolution. I have written a number of articles about him and am including one or more of these here, as well as articles written by my friend, Faye Axford, who is a historian at Athens, Alabama.

Abner was born on his father John Alloway Strange's plantation, Oak Hill, in Fluvanna County, Virginia. He settled in Limestone County, Alabama in the summer of 1825. Abner was the father of 19 children by two of his three wives. Our ancestor was his first wife, Elizabeth Ann Mitchell.

As I have previously mentioned, Charles and Ann Bernard's daughter, Sarah Catherine Bernard McCuan — my great-great-grandmother — lived with her daughter, Mary Ellender McCuan Johnson — my great-grandmother — during her elderly years. My grandmother, Lucy Lavinia Johnson Lindsey, remembered many stories that she told about her people and passed these on to me when I was a boy.

One of her stories was especially fascinating. This was about one of Great-Great Grandmother's great aunts being captured by the Indians soon after they moved into the wilderness (then Goochland County, Virginia). I was never able to find anything about this — and finally discounted it. I had somehow assumed that she was referring to her Strange family side. However, only recently I learned that she was, in fact, telling about her father Charles Bernard's Great Grand-Aunt Elizabeth. Elizabeth was the daughter of John Bernard Sr. and Mary Abney Bernard. They moved into the wilderness (Goochland County) when Elizabeth was a small child. Soon afterward, they were raided by the Indians (believed to have been Shawnees). Little Elizabeth was captured and was never seen or heard of again. This terrible story of our family's frontier life was passed down to each generation. I remember so well my Grandmother Lindsey telling of the Indian raid and how expeditions were sent out by the settlers in attempts to find the child.

Now, back to our Strange family. The attached charts, as you note, takes our family back to the Island of Pamona in the Orkney Islands, Scotland, as early as 1148 A.D. Our Strange family was originally of Celtic origin. However, because of the numerous raids on the island, they were eventually mixed with Norwegian bloods. The records in Scotland were derived from Scotland land records and do not show the first names of most of the generations. However, our lineage in this family was fortunate enough to have inherited the Strange Family land grant, therefore, we can trace our lineage back to John Strange of Ronaldsay, Scotland. He was born about 1332 A.D. William Alloway Strange (our direct ancestor) and his brother Robert were the first of our Strange Family to settle in America in 1635. However, our William had first arrived at Jamestown in 1619. He returned to Scotland in 1623, married and came back to Virginia in 1635 on the ship *Pauline*.

All of this is shown on the following charts and in the attached narratives.

William Lindsey McDonald

Great-Grand-Aunt Rebecca Ann McCuan was the oldest child of Nelson and Sarah Catherine Bernard McCua⁻. She married a Confederate soldier. As Aunt Maggie used to say, "He was passing through." He was William F. Graham, and their marriage was recorded in the family Bible on the date, "January 16, 1863." I don't know what happened to this marriage, or to Mr. Graham. I do know there was one daughter, Eliza. The Lauderdale County 1880 Census lists her as S. C., and she was known as Lena in Concrete City, Texas, where she is buried.

Our family knew Rebecca Ann as "Aunt Becky Ann." Uncle Isaac Mitchell McCuan's daughter, Blanche Kyle of McCrory, Arkansas, lived with her Aunt Rebecca Ann for a short time in Waco, Texas, after her mother died and before her daddy remarried. She referred to her Aunt Rebecca Ann as "Aunt Can." The 1870 Lauderdale County, Alabama, census shows Sarah Catherine McCuan, Rebecca Ann Graham, and daughter, Eliza Graham living with my great-grandparents, F. P. and Mary Ellender McCuan Johnson, at the old Cypress Cotton Mill near Florence. Next door, lived Martin B. Leach, a worker in the mill who was boarding with the neighbor. Soon after the census, Aunt Rebecca Ann married Martin B. Leach and moved to Allsboro, Alabama. I always wondered why, and it wasn't until recently that I learned. This information came to me by a pleasant visit from Rebecca Ann's great-grandson, William Speckels, his wife, Ruth, and son, Wade. Bill Speckels is president of a bank in El Campo, Texas. Ruth is a teacher. They told me that Martin Leach's people were natives of Tishamingo County, Mississippi, which is only a half mile or so west of Allsboro, Alabama. About 1880, a number of the Leach families in the area moved by wagons to Texas, including Aunt Rebecca Ann and her family. Aunt Becky Ann and Martin Leach had three children while living at Allsboro: Lucy, Ida, and Charlie. Two other daughters were born after they arrived in Texas: Lillie and Emma.

The story of the marriage of Aunt Becky's daughter Lillie to my Great-Uncle Robert McCuan Johnson is most interesting, and sad. I've heard it from the earliest days of my youth from my grandmother as well as from my Great-Aunt Maggie. Uncle Robert was a railroad man, and while traveling out west with the railroad, he visited his aunt, Rebecca Ann Leach at Waco, Texas. He fell in love with his first cousin, Lillie Leach, and married her. They had a son, Robert McCuan Johnson Jr. However, Uncle Robert abandoned Lillie while Robert Jr. was a small child. I have a copy of a letter written to my family by Lillie pleading with Robert to come back. "He told me he was going home and would send for me..." she wrote. "I wish you could see the baby; he is calling for Robert now...saying, 'Papa back, back.'"

Uncle Robert never returned to Texas or to Lillie and Robert Jr. He later married Clara Hendrix in Illinois, and they had a son, Roscoe Howard, who died in 1917.

Bill and Ruth Speckels told me that their Great-Aunt Lillie had a second son, Norris Martin Johnson, who was born October 9, 1903, some four months following Lillie's sad letter quoted above (dated June 10, 1903). My family never mentioned this second child. Surely they must have known.

Lillie's second marriage was to J. F. Turner, just a little while after Robert left her. Their (Lillie and J. F. Turner) first child, Alien Turner, was born May 5, 1904.

After studying these bits of information, I now suspect that Uncle Robert, who was gone for weeks at a time with his work on the railroad, probably came home and found Lillie pregnant with a child that he might have thought, was not his. This, I think, may have been why he left and never returned.

Anyhow, poor Lillie had a tragic life. She and J. F. Turner had five children, and all of them died young (some of them died "in their sleep," according to reports). Norris Martin Johnson died on April 29, 1908, at the age of five years. Her only child to live to be grown was Robert M. Johnson Jr. Incidentally, Lillie and J. F. Turner lived at San Francisco, California. Later, she married a Rickard and, according to Bill Speckels, died while riding on the back of a motorcycle in San Antonia, Texas, where she is buried.

My family always looked for Robert M. Johnson Jr. For some reason, they expected him to one day show up at Florence. His father, my Great-Uncle Robert Johnson Sr., died of a heart attack in the railroad yard at Chattanooga on August 10, 1915. They brought him to Florence for burial in the Florence Cemetery. He was placed in an expensive cast iron casket, air-sealed and with a glass top over his face so that Robert M. Johnson Jr. could one day dig up his father and see his face. This never happened. He never came to Florence. Aunt Maggie would say, too, "When Robert Jr. comes; we'll probably lose this home." I never understood what she meant and I still wonder.

In the 1930s, Judge Simpson of Florence was on a tour of the West and, while purchasing gasoline at a station in California, met Robert Johnson Jr. who owned the station. Robert asked the judge to call his aunts when he returned home. Judge Simpson called Aunt Maggie, but by then had forgotten the name of the small town where he had met Robert. Until this day, we do not know what happened to Robert Jr. Even the Speckels do not know. One thing is for sure, if he had children, they are the only living members of our Johnson family who still carry on that wonderful name that has meant so much to all of us — Johnson.

Great-Great-Aunt Martha Harriett McCuan married William L. Toon, a Confederate soldier. They had two daughters, Willie and Mary Elizabeth. Willie died young while visiting her grandmother, Sarah Catherine McCuan, at the Cypress Mills near Florence. She is buried at what is now the Florence Golf and Country Club on Cypress Creek alongside her Grandmother McCuan and my other Great-Great-Grandmother Martha Nichols Johnson. Mary Elizabeth married Newton Starkey of Limestone County. Cousin Newt was a prosperous businessman in the community of Cairo. Their house is still standing but the Starkey mill and other buildings have disappeared.

There is another family story that I heard many, many times. It was always exciting and, as a small boy, I could almost picture the adventure of our family. The story begins with the visit of a drummer to our Great-Grandmother Mary Ellender McCuan Johnson's home on Sweetwater Avenue at Florence. As was the custom in those days, Grandma invited him to sit at their table. While eating, he mentioned that he had just come from Cairo in Limestone County. Grandma perked up, saying that she had a sister, Martha, at Cairo and had lost contact with her. As luck would have it, he had, in fact, been to Martha's house.

He told them exactly where to find that lovely person whom we have come to know as Aunt Pattie.

And so it was that a caravan was organized in the summer of 1909 with our family, the Johnsons, and Aunt Lucy's family, the Statoms. It took, according to the saga, two days to get there. They camped the first night at a spring on Bluewater Creek. What a sight it must have been as they arrived at Cairo. Aunt Pattie was at church, as there was a summer meeting in progress.

Cousin Nelson Starkey was a small boy. He remembered the trip and that exciting visit as long as he lived. He told me that he thought it was a Gypsy caravan and ran to hide in the barn. His brother Carlos was sent to the Methodist Church to fetch Aunt Pattie. She came across the hill, according to our family story, singing and shouting! After this visit in the summer of 1909, our families became very close and visited quite often. My Grandmother Lindsey and her family would ride a train from Sheffield to Athens, and Cousin New Starkey would meet their train in his buggy and take them to Cairo for a week's visit.

THE STRANGE AND BERNARD FAMILY BIBLES

THE STRANGE FAMILY BIBLE

Abner Alloway Strange removed the family record pages from his Bible and attached them to his application for pension submitted December 10, 1832. The originals are in the National Archives and Records Building, Washington, D.C. These papers are in a very bad condition because of their age; hence, it is impossible to make out all the entries. The first page was apparently torn in two; it contains the names of children by his first wife, Elizabeth. The second page shows the children by his second wife, Mary, whom he called "Polly."

Entries on first page, left column:

Gideon M. Strange, Eldest son of Abner A. and Elizabeth Strange was born 17th May 1783

Judith Strange, daughter of the same

Thomas Strange

Abner Strange

Milley Strange

John Strange

Rebecca F. Strange

Ellen Strange

Ann M. Strange

First page, right column

Martha M. Strange, daughter of Abner A. & Eliz Strange was born September 4, 1799

John M. Flanagan son of Simpson and Martha M. Flanagan was born January 24, 1822

Abner Flanagan son of (words llegible) was born April 21st 1827.

(other entries not legible — end of first page)

Second page

Abner & Polly A. Strange his wife was married the 10th day of December 1805.

Harriet Vanison Strange, Daughter of the above was born the 22nd of December in the year of our Lord 1806.

Elizabeth Mitchell Strange, Daughter of the above was born the 2nd day of July in the year of our Lord 1808.

Jamima Vanison Strange, daughter of the above was born the 12th day of July in the year of our Lord 1810.

(The next name is not legible. The only words that can be read are: "was born the 5th day of June 1812.")

Archiles Mitchell Strange son of Abner & Polly A. Strange was born the 23rd day of May 1814.

George Strange son of Abner A. & Polly S. Strange was born the 23rd day of July 1816.

(The next entry is not legible. The only words that can be read are: "Strange, Daughter of above was born 17th day of February 1817.")

Edward Saunders Strange son of the above was born 14 day of March 1821.

Sarah Jane Strange Daughter of the above was born 4th day of September 1825.

THE BERNARD FAMILY BIBLE

This is the family Bible of Abner's daughter, Ann Mitchell Alloway Strange, and her husband, Charles M. Bernard. It is in very good condition and is owned now by the writer, William Lindsey McDonald. Ann was a conscientious record keeper. She recorded the births, marriages, and deaths of her brothers and sisters and their children, her father, grandfather, mother-in-law, her children and grandchildren. The Bible was published in Philadelphia in 1811 by Mathew Carey, No. 122 Market Street. It was brought to Alabama from Virginia by the family in 1825. The Bible was inherited by Ann's daughter Sarah Catherine Bernard who married Nelson McCuan of Limestone County, Alabama. Sarah Catherine recorded the births, marriages, and deaths of her family and completely filled the remaining available space in the Bible. She brought the Bible with her when she moved to Lauderdale County, Alabama, after her husband's death in 1864. At her death, the Bible was inherited by her daughter, Mary Ellender McCuan, who married Franklin Pierce Johnson of Lauderdale County. When Mary Ellender died August 29, 1924, the Bible was inherited by her eldest child, Magnolia Johnson, widow of Martin Cole. Before her death in 1962, Magnolia Johnson Cole gave the Bible to William Lindsey McDonald, the grandson of her deceased sister Lucy Johnson (wife of Leonard Lindsey of Lauderdale County).

ENTRIES IN THE BERNARD BIBLE:

FAMILY RECORD

MARRIAGES   (first page)

Charles M. Bernard & Ann Mitchell Alloway Strange his wife was married the 1st day Feby 1812.

Jarret M. Ridgeway and Ann M. Bernard his wife was married the 2nd of October 1836.

Nelson McCuan and Sarah Catherine Bernard was married March the 9th 1843.

James H. Jones and Martha H. Bernard was married January the 30th 1844.

William L. Toon and Martha H. McCuan was married December the 18 1862.

George F. Graham and Rebecka Ann McCuan was married January the 15, 1863.

John C. Harrison and Ann M. Bernard was married February the 23d 1841.

Charles Burnes and Mary Suffrosy Harrison was married January the 16th 1845.

FAMILY RECORD   (page 2)

BIRTHS

Charles M. Bernard was born the 11th day of February 1788

Ann M. A. Strange wife of C. M. Bernard was born the 26th day of January 1797

Abner Allen Bernard son of Charles M. Bernard and Ann his wife was born the 8th day of Feb. 1814

Elizabeth Ann Cooper daughter of Jacob and Elleaner Cooper was born the 16th day of September 1813

John Cooper son of Jacob and Elleaner Cooper was born the 3rd day of February 1811

Mary Elizabeth Bernard daughter C. M. and Ann M. Bernard was born the 26th Aug't 1816

Treana Ellender Bernard daughter of C. M. and Ann Bernard was born the 9th day of December 1818

BIRTHS

Ann Mitchell Bernard was born the 2nd day February 1821

Martha Harriett Bernard was born July 17, 1824

Sarah Catherine Bernard was born September 27th 1827

(penmanship changed at this point)

James Michael Jones son of James and Martha M. Jones was born January the 19th 1845

Rebecca Ann McCuan daughter of Nelson and Sarah C. McCuan was born March the 11th 1844

Samuel T. McCuan son of Nelson and Sarah C. McCuan was born February the 7th 1846

Martha H. McCuan daughter of Nelson and Sarah C. McCuan was born January the 25th 1847

FAMILY RECORD   (page 3)

BIRTHS

Martha Delila Burns was born

Martha Delila Burns daughter of Charles and Mary S. Burns was born November the 30th 1845

Jas Biship was Born October the 19th 1838

Roseanah Elizabeth McCuan daughter of Nelson and Sarah McCuan was born April the 7th 1850

DEATHS

Elizabeth A Strange mother of Ann M. Bernard departed this life 22nd January 1803

John A. Strange Grandfather of Ann M. Bernard departed this life _____ day of _____

Ellenior Cooper sister of A.M. Bernard and wife of Jacob Cooper departed this life 2nd day of May 1816

BIRTHS

John W McCuan son of Nelson and Sarah McCuan was born the 27th day of September 1853

Mary Ellender McCuan daughter of N and S McCuan was born the 21 day of Sep 1856

DEATHS

Gideon A Strange Brother of A M Bernard departed this life the ____ day of _____

Judith A Strange Sister of Ann M. Bernard departed this life ____ day of _____

Mildred A. Strange Sister of Ann M. Bernard departed this life _____ day of _____

FAMILY RECORD   (page 4)

DEATHS

John Godeon Strange son of Abner A. Strange (Jr) and Salley his wife departed this life the 20th of September 1825 at 2 o'clock in the morning

Mary Lucy A. Strange daughter of A. A. Strange Jr and Salley his wife departed this life Wednesday the 21st of September 1825

Abner A Strange departed this life July the 22 1826

Abner A Strange Senior departed this life the 27th day of August 1834

(penmanship changed at this point)

Thomas M. A. Strange departed this life the 18th day December 1855

John William McCuan A son of Nelson and Sarah McCuan departed this life September the 25, 1858 age 4 years and 11 months and 29 days

Martha Delila Burnes Daughter of Charles and Mary S. Burnes departed this life March the 23d 1846 aged 3 months and 24 days

Charles M. Bernard departed this life July the 15th 1827

Samuel T. McCuan departed this life the 3d of March 1846 ages 3 weeks and 3 days

Abner Allen Bernard departed this life the 11th of June 1848 aged 34 years 4 months and 6 days

John C. Harrison departed this life the 15th day of July 1856

DEATHS

(END OF PAGE 4 AND END OF BERNARD FAMILY BIBLE RECORDS)

EXCERPTS FROM THE WILL OF ABNER ALLOWAY STRANGE, LIMESTONE COUNTY, ALABAMA

This will is dated July 29, 1834, and is recorded in Volume 4 of Wills, pages 391-392, Office of the Probate Judge, Limestone County, Alabama.

"...I give to and bequeath to my beloved wife all my land and possessions where I now live..."

"...I give and bequeath to my daughter Nancy Ann Bernard one parcel of land more or less beginning at..."

"...I give and bequeath all my lands and money, coming to me in Virginia to be equally divided amongst all my children that is to say, Thomas M. Strange, Nancy Ann Bernard, Martha M. Flanagan, Harriet V. Harvey, Elizabeth M. Strange, Mary M. Burns, Jemima M. Elum, Archie M. Strange, and Sarah Jane Strange..."

"...Abner A. Strange's[19] heirs has had their part of my estate. Also, Eleanor Cooper's heirs has had their part of my estate..."

THE EDWARD SANDERS STRANGE BIBLE

Edward Sanders (or Saunders) Strange, born March 14, 1821, was the eighteenth child of the Revolutionary War soldier, Abner Alloway Strange. He lived and left descendants in Limestone County, Alabama. He donated the land and material and helped build the Salem Methodist Church, which stands only a few miles from the grave of his father, Abner A. Strange. Edward married twice. His youngest child, Nellie Dupree Strange (the wife of Audie M. Christopher), lives in the Salem community. She is a granddaughter of the Revolutionary War soldier, possibly the only living actual granddaughter of a Revolutionary War soldier in the state of Alabama. She owns the Edward Sanders Strange Bible.

Entries in the Edward Sanders Strange Bible

Edward S. Strange and Mary A. Strange his wife was married December 18, 1845.

Edward S. Strange and Mary F. Strange his wife were married January 30, 1889.

Audie M. Christopher and Nellie D. Strange were married July 19, 1914.

Margaret Lula Strange married John R. Witt. Mary Alice Strange married William Jones; second marriage to John Jones.

BIRTHS

George Simpson Strange was born December 18, 1846

John Baty Strange was born January 28, 1849

Lucuis Faine Strange was born April 13, 1851

Andrew Harding Strange was born February 13, 1853

Edward Sanders Strange was born March 14, 1821

Mary Ann Strange was born June 11, 1823

Mary Alice Strange was born April 9, 1857

Margret Lula Strange was born May 18, 1859

William Edward Strange was born October 12, 1861

Edward Sanders Strange was born September 11, 1855

Benton Sanders Strange was born November 11, 1889

Nellie Dupree Strange was born April 17, 1893

DEATHS

Edward Sanders Strange departed this life June 23, 1856*

Mary Strange departed this life April 13, 1860

John Baty Strange departed this life July 7, 1879

George Simpson Strange departed this life August 23, 1881 1/2 past 11 o'clock

Lucuis Faine Strange departed this life August 19, 1884   6 o'clock a.m.

William Edward Strange departed this life December 19, 1884

Nancy Ann Strange departed this life April 26, 1886

Edward Sanders Strange departed this life October 20, 1900**

Mollie Strange Holland, September 25, 1938

Mary Alice Jones, December 31, 1939

* Edward Sanders Strange Jr. (writer's note).

** Edward Sanders Strange Sr., son of Abner Alloway Strange (writer's note).

CHILDREN AND DESCENDANTS OF

ANN MITCHELL ALLOWAY STRANGE AND HER HUSBAND CHARLES M. BERNARD

A. CHILDREN

1. Abner Allen Bernard, born May 8, 1811; died June 11, 1848

2. Mary Elizabeth Bernard, born August 24, 1816; died September 14, 1825

3. Treana Ellender Bernard, born December 9, 1818

4. Ann Mitchell Bernard, born February 2, 1821; married Jarret M. Ridgeway

5. Martha Harriet Bernard, born July 14, 1826; married James H. Jones

6. Sarah Catherine Bernard, born September 27, 1827; married Nelson McCuan

B. CHILDREN OF SARAH CATHERINE BERNARD AND HER HUSBAND NELSON McCUAN

1. Rebecca Ann McCuan, born March 11, 1844; married George F. Graham

2. Samuel T. McCuan, born February 7, 1846; died March 3, 1846

3. Martha H. McCuan born January 25, 1847; died August 30, 1929. She married William L. Toon. They had two daughters — Willie (who died young) and Mary Elizabeth (February 24, 1867 - August 1, 1949). Mary Elizabeth married Newton Allen Starkey (1859-1924). They had the following children:

> William Haywood — married Clema Irene Furgerson
>
> Walter Arnett — married Beulah French Kin
>
> Winford Carlos — married Eda Jane Adams
>
> Nelson Rivers — married Bessie Pearl Underwood
>
> Beulah Lynn — married Edward W. Tuten
>
> Lucy Auleria — married Hal Sherbert
>
> Leona O'Neal — married Newton Davis (second Charles Stinnett)
>
> Cassie Lorine — married Cleo Laughmiller

4. John William McCuan, born September 27, 1853; died September 26, 1858

5. Marry Ellender McCuan, born September 24, 1856; died August 29, 1924. She married Franklin Pierce Johnson (March 20, 1854 - October 26, 1926) of Lauderdale County, Alabama. They had the following children:

> Magnolia (December 21, 1874 - February 19, 1962); married Martin Cole
>
> Roscoe Johnson (April 4, 1877 - November 22, 1911)
>
> Robert M. Johnson (July 2, 1879 - August 10, 1915); married Clara Hendricks

George Elliot (September 17, 1881 - September 9, 1957);
married Molly Pattie

Lucy Lavinia Johnson (April 23, 1885 - October 30, 1951);
married Leonard Lindsey (January 21, 1878 - May 30,   1960)[20]

Fred Johnson (April 23, 1890 - 1892)

Freddie Lee (July 20, 1892 - June 27, 1956); married Acy Watson

Effie Odell (September 2, 1903 -)

6. Roseana Elizabeth McCuan, born April 7, 1850

7. Isaac Mitchell McCuan, born September 23, 1858; died in McCrory, Arkansas.

8. Lucy Francis McCuan, born January 28, 1862; died June 28, 1932. She married James A. Statom. They had five children:

Maude Obedience — married Robert Minor

Ollie Mitchell — married Lovie Sharp

Virgil E. — married Myrtle Blakely

James Chalmer — married Ida Zahnd

John Price — married Muncie Sharp

FOOTNOTES

1. Application for pension, Limestone County, Alabama. December 10, 1832. Original copy in the National Archives and Records Building, Washington, D.C.

2. Ibid. Also, Bernard Family Bible

3. Ibid. Also, Will of John A. Strange, dated June 7, 1810, Will book No. 2 o. s. pages 89-91 Court of Fluvanna County, Virginia. Also, old church records of Fluvanna County, Virginia.

4. BIOGRAPHICAL AND HISTORICAL SKETCHES OF THE STRANGES OF AMERICA AND ACROSS THE SEAS, compiled by Alexander Taylor Strange, 1911.

5. Recorded November 26, 1635 in Charles City County, Virginia.

6. Will Book 2 o. s. pages 89-81, Court of Fluvanna County, Virginia.

7. Vol 4 of Wills, pages 391-392, Office of Probate Judge, Limestone County, Alabama.

8. HISTORY OF ALABAMA AND DICTIONARY OF ALABAMA BIOGRAPHY VOL IV, by Thomas M. Owen, page 1632, published 1921.

9. Bernard Family Bible.

10. Grandfather of the late Captain Archiles (Billy) Strange of Athens, Alabama, who died about 1962 near 90 years of age. Cap' Strange was instrumental in directing the writer to the grave and home of Abner Alloway Strange.

11. The writer has Ann's black bonnet that she brought from Virginia "for Sunday occasions." The writer inherited this bonnet from his grandmother Lucy Johnson Lindsey, Ann's great-granddaughter.

12. A rock was removed from the large kitchen fireplace in 1960 and placed in the writer's kitchen fireplace at Carter Acres Farm, Florence, Alabama.

13. A. A. Strange applied for a pension December 10, 1832. He was granted a lump sum payment of $100 and was given $40 annually. He did not live to collect more than three years of this pension (Volume XIV Sen

Doc 514 23rd Congress 1st Session 1833-34 — Revolutionary War Pension Rolls).

14. Mary Saunders Strange applied for a pension as a widow of a Revolutionary War veteran on October 4, 1858, at Athens, Alabama.

15. Erected by the writer in 1960. The field where the grave is located is owned by John Moss of Limestone County, Alabama.

16. Abner stated in his pension application that his older brother Abraham had his father's family Bible.

17. Colonel Gideon A. Strange of Fluvanna County, Virginia, served General Lafayette as a private escort on his second visit to America. Colonel Strange was seriously wounded in the Battle of Palo Alta in Mexico and died of blood poisoning and lockjaw while convalescing at his home in Fluvanna County, Virginia.

18. Dated June 7, 1810 (pages 89-91 of Will Book No. 2 o. s., Court of Fluvanna County, Virginia).

19. His son, Abner Jr.

20. Grandparents of the writer — Lucy Johnson and Leonard Lindsey. They had nine children:

> Carmel Lindsey, born December 11, 1903; married
> Hardy R. Springer
>
> Carlos Lindsey, born February 17, 1907; married
> Katherine Boyd
>
> Pauline Myran Lindsey, born March 15, 1910; died
> March 6, 1964; married William Ervin
McDonald (born November 1, 1903)
>
> Lura Lindsey, born August 12, 1912; married James
> F. Hall Sr.
>
> Nelson McCuan Lindsey, born March 26, 1915;
married Mary Mason

Howard Shannon Lindsey, born April 29, 1917; married Lorine Sutton

Marvin Glenn Lindsey, born November 4, 1919; married Betty Jean Gullett of Tennessee

Claud Raymond Lindsey, born April 24, 1922

Mary Ellen Lindsey, born June 12, 1928.

Appendix 2 – Clan Donald

It Is No Joy Without Clan Donald

"Ni h-eibhneas gan Chlainn Domhnaill" is and ancient maxim among our clansman in the Celtic language of our ancestors. In our English translation this means "It is no joy without Clan Donald." This speaks of the tie that binds our family together. This was one of the first things I learned as a boy, living in the same house with my grandfather, seeing and being a part of the loyalty that bonded all branches of our large family. My grandfather and his brothers, although separated by mountains and prairies, maintained close ties throughout the long span of their years. I find this same and considerable covenant among my own brothers and sister. I was not surprised to find these same ties in Scotland where we were so warmly greeted and welcomed to the home of our ancestors. "It is no joy without Clan Donald," is surely a part of our inbred genes from ancient days when all McDonalds lived together as one great clan of Domhnaills.

This following essay was written by Amy McDonald to help comfort her father, Tom McDonald, after the death of two of his brothers, Johnny and Bobby. Both died within a two month span.

The Eastern Gate

It is only as we grow older that the passing of time matters...that it actually registers as something lost. We really don't have all the time in the world.

I consider myself blessed to have been born into the McDonald family...this McDonald clan. These are ties forged not only by blood, but by loyalty, commitment, kindness, faith, and love...so much love.

Being children of the youngest brother, Will and I have been recipients of a multitude of family stories. My favorites have always been the ones of the brothers and sister growing up together. Exploits would probably be a better description...tales that leave me laughing no matter how many times I hear them. But the amazing thing, the very unique thing, about this family is that it didn't stop there. The brothers and sister grew up, married, had children and passed it on. Passed what on? They taught their children, grandchildren, great-grandchildren, nieces, and nephews...us...what family is all about.

I always remember the Christmas parties...Uncle Bill saying the blessing...summer reunions...Sunday afternoon gatherings. We all remember those. But the most memorable glimpses to me of what makes this family so special have been in the quieter, more day-to-day moments. Brothers and sister eating Wednesday morning breakfast...playing dulcimers...visiting each other...supporting and caring for each other in the best and worst of times. What an example they have set. It is an example that challenges me to focus on relationships, to stop wasting precious time, and to realize that when the storms of life pass over and through us, it will be family that is left standing.

We have amongst us survivors of the Great Depression, World War II veterans, Army, Navy, and Air Force veterans, historians, carpenters, artists, nurses, and teachers. They have lived lives of honor and perseverance...lives of service to their country, families, neighbors, and friends. In my eyes, they truly are the "Greatest Generation."

In my lifetime, I can only hope that my life reflects the hard work of Daddy Ervin, the sweet nature of Mama Pauline...how I wish I had known her...the integrity of Uncle Bill, the laughter of Uncle Joe, the quiet understanding of Uncle Dan, the toughness of Uncle Bobby, the kindheartedness of Aunt Virginia, the gentle spirit of Uncle Johnny, and the compassionate strength of Tom, my father. I am so fortunate to be able to say that my grandparents, aunts, and uncles have made a difference in my life. But blessings such as these are also shadowed with the sorrow that comes from loss...such deep loss. It is in times like these that the realities of our existence on this earth are hard to accept. Life is fragile...it is short...and it is precious.

The only consolation I can sometimes find when facing death is knowing that in spite of the separation now, there will be a reunion later. Uncle Bill said something recently that has given me so much comfort and peace. A few days before Uncle Johnny's death, Uncle Bill said, "Brother, I'll meet you at the Eastern gate." Through this season of tears, we can rest assured that those we have lost are not alone...they were welcomed and embraced at the Eastern gate. What a reunion that must have been...and what a reunion that awaits each of us.

Legacies are things passed from generation to generation...and their legacy is immense. It says, "Stand strong...take heart...stick together...remember your heritage...pass it on." And always at the end, it says, "I'll meet you at the Eastern gate."

Amy McDonald

September, 2006

McDonald Family

From left: Bobby McDonald, Joe McDonald, Virginia Lindsey, Johnny McDonald, William Ervin McDonald (father), William L. McDonald, Dan McDonald and kneeling, Tom McDonald

Appendix 3 DNA Testing

This appendix consists of a copy of a certificate of DNA testing on the author, William Lindsey McDonald and several pieces of email. The e-mail correspondences should explain the significance of the results of the DNA testing.

GENOGRAPHIC

Certificate of Y-chromosome DNA testing

In recognition of your participation in the Genographic Project, we hereby certify that

William Lindsey McDonald

belongs to:

Haplogroup R1a (M17)

The designations for all twelve loci examined for this purpose are listed here, along with the Short Tandem Repeats (STRs) outcome for each.

393	19	391	439	389-1	389-2	388	390	426	385a	385b	392
13	15	11	10	14	18	12	26	12	11	14	11

September 25, 2005

THE WAITT FAMILY FOUNDATION

NATIONAL GEOGRAPHIC   IBM

----- Original Message -----
From: "David McDonald" <david.mcdonald@mindspring.com>
To: <lbmiddleton@charter.net>
Sent: Friday, September 23, 2005 8:27 PM
Subject: Family Tree DNA

William,

I received an email from Family Tree DNA on a match on the 12 and one off on the 25.
Where do you live? I'm in Georgia near Atlanta, our family here since the 1830's. Before
that they were in Laurens County SC. My ancestor from there is Alexander McDonald
born 1809

David McDonald

----- Original Message -----
From: "Lindsey Middleton" <lbmiddleton@charter.net>
To: "David McDonald" <david.mcdonald@mindspring.com>
Sent: Friday, September 23, 2005 11:22 PM
Subject: Re: Family Tree DNA

Hello David,

My name is Lindsey Middleton, and I am the granddaughter of William (Daddy Bill to
me) McDonald. He is in his late 70's and doesn't "do" email, so I've been helping him
manage the technical side of the DNA testing process. He is in Florence, Alabama, and
I'm a little closer to you over here in Auburn.

Daddy Bill is an accomplished historian and genealogist (he is actually the City Historian
in Florence) and has even published a local book called "History of Clan McDonald"
(1994). I got out the book when I received your email this evening, and the first ancestor
he lists is John McDonald (1792-1860), who brought our branch of the family to
Alabama, leaving South Carolina sometime between 1816 and 1819. I also see that his
wife Margaret is thought to be the daughter of Stephen Emory of Laurens County, so it
seems pretty clear that we share some common ancestry.

I know that Daddy Bill has some family information that dates back to the immigration
from Scotland sometime around 1745 from Knoch Bay on the Isle of Skye. There is an
assumption of a direct line to Somerled (but I would imagine most McDonalds claim that,
right?), and that was one of the reasons he wanted to do the genetic testing through
Family Tree DNA. His health is not good, as he suffers from Parkinson's, as well as
macular degeneration, and as the father of two daughters, he wanted to complete the Y37
test and gather as much information as he can, while he is still able.

I will call him in the morning and let him know that the two of you have matched. I am sure that he would be pleased to speak to you over the phone, and he receives regular requests from people seeking genealogical information, so I would imagine he could mail you copies of any records you might be interested in. Do you have any information and/or clues that predate what you know about your ancestor Alexander?

Well, it should be exciting to see if the two of you together can add some pieces to the puzzle. I'm sure we will be in touch soon.

Best regards,
Lindsey Middleton

----- Original Message -----
From: "David McDonald" <david.mcdonald@mindspring.com>
To: "Lindsey Middleton" <lb.middleton@charter.net>
Sent: Saturday, September 24, 2005 6:59 AM
Subject: Re: Family Tree DNA

Hi Lindsey,

Good to hear from you. It would be great to hear from your grandfather. Just looking at census records for Laurens Co. for 1810 I see a John McDonald (John McDonal I think it is spelled in census) that from the census brackets seems to have born 1755-1765. He appears to match up as Alexander. Maybe your John was his son and your John was my Alexander's brother. Actually only about 20% of McDonalds match up with the Chiefs and are descended from Somerled through the male line. But your grandfather and I do match up with that line. Not to get technical but there are a few extra mutations on my Y DNA that are slightly different from most of the other chiefly lines. The guys at Family Tree DNA seems to think it was a one time jump of several of the markers. Since your grandfather seems to share these I think it is a indication we are close. If it is OK would you load the info into the Y DNA part of the Family Tree DNA website. Here is my contact info.

David McDonald
5805 Millers Pond Lane
Powder Springs, GA 30127

Home Phone 770 439-8469
Cell 770 401-5081
Work 404 714-0776

From: "Lindsey Middleton" <lbmiddleton@charter.net>
To: "David McDonald" <david.mcdonald@mindspring.com>
Sent: Sunday, September 25, 2005 5:45 PM
Subject: Re: Family Tree DNA

> Hello again, David,
>
> I spoke with Daddy Bill, and he is very excited about your genetic match.
> I have explained to him my very limited understanding of what the testing
> has shown us so far, but I have the feeling you could explain things a
> little better yourself. Would you mind terribly giving him a call? His
> contact information is as follows:
>
> William L McDonald
> 2207 Berry Avenue
> Florence, AL 35630
> (256) 766-3872
>
> I see from your previous email that you have several contact numbers, and
> I'm guessing you might have a few more constraints on your time than he
> does. Probably the only major parameter for him is that he usually goes to
> bed in the 7 o'clock hour (CST), so you'd do better to call him during the
> day.
>
> Truly, he feels that the connection with you is a minor miracle. So much of
> genealogy is based on leaps of faith & deductive reasoning, so to have some
> concrete ties means a great deal to him. To tell you the truth, he had a
> lurking fear that the testing would show that he's not really a McDonald
> after all, so at least now we know that all the mothers in his ancestral
> line were faithful! My grandparents, my mother, a first cousin, and I have
> each been to Scotland on what might be considered our own version of a
> pilgrimage, so we are all excited to learn more about our forebears.
>
> As you suggested, I entered in the individual values on the Family Tree yDNA
> section, as well as the ysearch site & National Geographic's Genographic
> project site. I notice that on ysearch, the two records that match most
> closely to Daddy Bill (User ID #s: DWGYR & JSVTW, his User ID is QGAUX) list
> the contact person as David McDonald. Are one or both of those connected to
> you? I'm still trying to piece together all the connections and what the
> marker values represent, so any tips you could offer about interpreting them
> would be great.
>
> Well, Daddy Bill is looking forward to hearing from you!
>
> Thanks so much,

Appendix 4 - Glencoe
Glencoe

There is no more tragic massacre in the history of mankind than was suffered by our family at Glencoe. According to the traditions of our family, each generation is supposed to tell the newer generations about the treachery of the Campbell Clan and what they did to our McDonalds. Here is our story, and I might introduce it by saying that I stood one day at Glencoe to feel the intense sadness of that night more than three hundred years ago when the Campbells slaughtered our people. Bagpipers met our bus and a small boy in a kilt handed Dorothy a bouquet of heather. We looked and remembered, and it did seem that I had been there before.

Following the accession of William III, the old problem of "pacification of the Highlands" came once more to the forefront. The Clan Chiefs who remained loyal to the exiled James VII were given a simple choice. They must take an oath of allegiance of William by January 1, 1692, or be crushed. The aged chief of the Glencoe McDonalds reluctantly made his way through ice and snow to Fort William, but was told that he must take an oath at Inveraray in the presence of the Sheriff or his deputy. When McDonald arrived at Inveraray on January 3rd, the deputy was absent and would not return until January 6th. Since McDonald's oath was a week late, it was technically invalid and his certificate was canceled at Edinburgh.

Hence, an example was to be made of the McDonalds whom were called "the only popish clan in the kingdom." Late in January, Robert Campbell of Glenlyon was dispatch to Glencoe with 120 men of the Campbell Clan.

There was an abiding tradition among the Scottish clans that even one's enemy must be sheltered and entertained during times of cruel ice and snowstorms. Thus, although the Campbells were ancient enemies, they were given shelter and entertained in the homes of the McDonalds. In the early morning hours of February 13, 1692, while the McDonalds were sleeping, the Campbells fell upon them and butchered men, women, and children. A few of some of the younger McDonalds managed, however, to escape in the surrounding hills to eventually tell the world of the horror of the night and how the Campbells had massacred the McDonalds. Our family has never forgotten, nor will ever forget the treachery by the Campbells.

William Lindsey McDonald

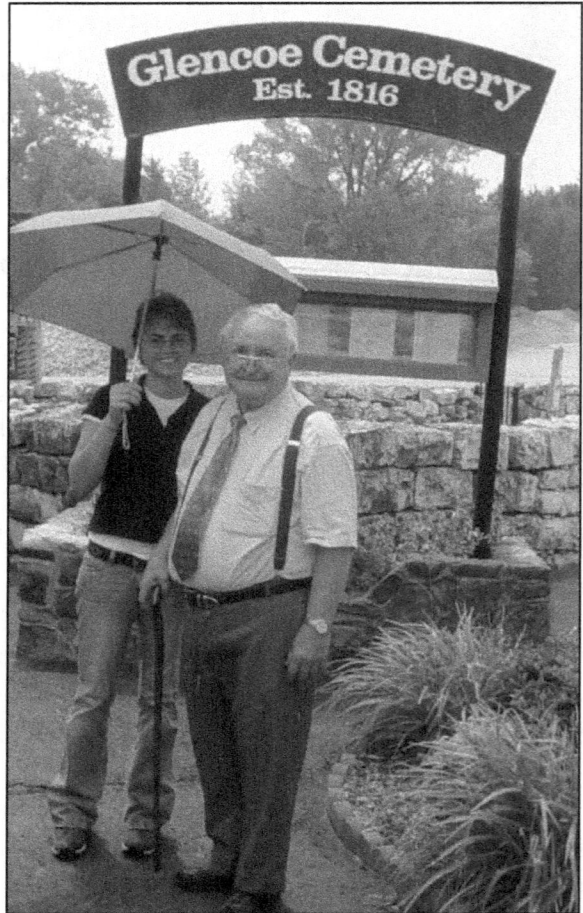

Appendix 5 – Soldier Boy in Blue
Soldier Boy in Blue

By William Lindsey McDonald

(This story is about a young militiaman whose father was a captain in the Newberry County, South Carolina, militia during the war with England. This information was told to the author by the late Elsie Lindsey Bradfoot, who was the great-great-granddaughter of John L. Lindsey.)

About the time that Thomas Gainsborough was creating his famous work, *The Blue Boy*, in England in 1770, a young boy in Newberry County, South Carolina, could easily have been used as a model for his painting. John L. Lindsey, born in Frederick County, Virginia, in 1764, persuaded his mother to cut out a coat that matched his father's regimental colors. This coat, along with a quilt stitched together by John L. Lindsey's daughter-in-law, remained in the Lindsey family until 1934, when they were both placed in the casket of David Lindsey.

Even though this lad was of the young age of 15 or 16, he served as an orderly for his father, Captain Samuel Lindsey, in the Revolutionary War, especially during the raids of the British soldiers against the American colonists in Newberry County, South Carolina. This occurred around 1779 and 1780. When his father marched away under the command of militia General Levi Casey and participated in the famous Battle of Kings Mountain, young John L. Lindsey was permitted to go along with his father as an orderly. It was remembered by members of the family that he actually participated in the fighting that occurred during his father's involvement in the Kings Mountain campaign.

John L. Lindsey was the grandson of Colonel John Lindsey of Frederick County, Virginia, who served as a colonial militiaman under General George Washington prior to the Revolutionary War. Colonel Lindsey had a number of sons. Four of his sons served as officers in the South Carolina militia during the campaign to protect the colonies from the invasion of British General Cornwallis. During the early years of the Revolutionary War, gangs of Tories who sided with England against the American colonies committed horrible atrocities against the patriots loyal to the American colonies in Newberry County. There was **great** conflict between the two groups of people living in that area. Members of the Lindsey clan were patriots and, according to family tradition, suffered greatly at the hands of the Tories in Newberry County. This probably had a lot to do with Captain Samuel Lindsey and his wife agreeing to allow young John L. Lindsey, in his boyhood years, to serve with his father in the South Carolina militia.

In 1818, John L. Lindsey with his wife Rebecca Anderson moved from Newberry County, South Carolina, to the area in Tennessee around Columbia. This was an attempt by him to acquire some of the land that had been granted to his father as a land grant for his service as an officer during the Revolutionary War. In 1826, we find him in Wayne County, Tennessee, where he acquired land along the Natchez Trace, almost on the Alabama-Tennessee state line. He became the first of the Lindsey clan that settled in and around the Muscle Shoals area during the opening of northwest Alabama following the treaties with the Chickasaw and Cherokee Indian Nations. The area where John L. Lindsey's home was built was at a place later known as Cypress Inn, Tennessee. At the time he came here and settled, it was known as Sixteen Mile House, denoting it was 16 miles from the Tennessee River. This was a post on the Natchez Trace that was operated by the Chickasaw Nation in agreement with the United States Army, which established what was later known as the Natchez Trace. Earlier, it had been operated by an Indian by the name of Tuscumbia. This Chickasaw name was later given to the city of Tuscumbia, Alabama.

The Lindsey clan married into families in what is now known as Lauderdale County, Alabama. One of the citizens of Cypress Inn, Grace Culver, in talking with the author, remembers the location of the Lindsey home on Cooper Creek, in the area known as Cypress Inn. Ms. Culver remembers the logs of this early log house were of chestnut and lay where they had fallen from the remains of the house during her early childhood. According to family legend, John L.

Lindsey either lived with his son Sylvester Lindsey and daughter-in-law Ellie in his older years, or his son and daughter-in-law lived with him in the family home. Sylvester and Ellie Lindsey had no children. There is a certificate in the Lindsey family showing that Sam Houston commissioned Sylvester a captain in the Tennessee militia in 1828. It is regarded as one of the Lindsey family heirlooms.

The author and a member of the Wood family, William Wood, did considerable research in attempting to locate what was known as Cooper Cemetery. Recently, this burial ground was pointed out to members of the McDonald family by residents of the Cypress Inn area. The gravesite of John L. Lindsey has been identified because of its location next to the grave of Sylvester Lindsey. In recent months, this grave of an American Revolutionary patriot has been marked by members of the McDonald, Wood, and Sego families. Its marking is dedicated as a monument to a young boy by the name of John L. Lindsey, who wore the coat of blue during his fifteenth and sixteenth years against invasion of the British Army into the southern colonies.

JOHN L. LINDSEY
1764 — CA 1830
REV. WAR VET (COWPEN)
ALSO WIFE
REBECCA ANDERSON

Marker placed on the grave of Revolutionary War veteran John L. Lindsey. The gravesite is near Cypress Inn, Tennessee and was finally located and marked in 2008.

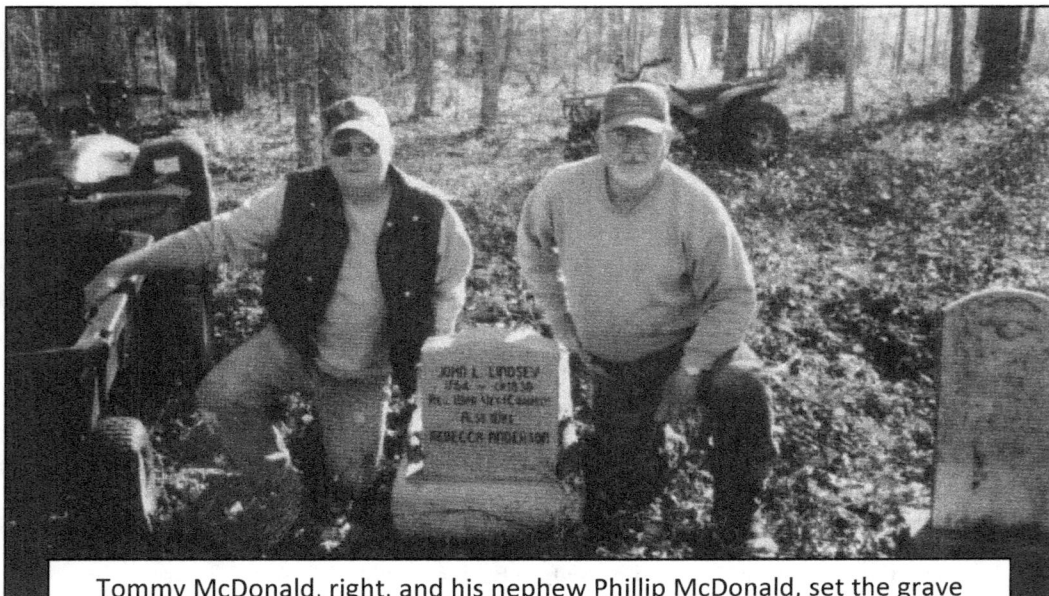

Tommy McDonald, right, and his nephew Phillip McDonald, set the grave marker for one of their ancestors, Revolutionary War veteran John L. Lindsey, at Cooper Cemetery on Wayne County, Tennessee, in the spring of 2008.

Appendix 6 – Worst Depression

The Worst of the Depression

Introduction: My niece, Amy McDonald, who teaches at Shades Valley in Birmingham, asked that I write a brief account of our family during the Great Depression.

Stewart L. Udall in his book "Quiet Crisis" describes this part of Alabama where we lived during the Great Depression:

"In no other region in the United States were there more families on relief or with lower incomes. The Tennessee Valley was one of the most depressed areas of the United States."

Mother and Dad were married by the North Wood Methodist pastor, Dr. J. F. Sturdivant, in the Church Parsonage.

Dad had previously been employed at Mr. Lewellan's Planning Mill, where they made caskets three shifts a day during the 1918 flu epidemic. During construction of Wilson Dam, Dad was employed first as a painter, welder, and later as a carpenter. Just prior to his marriage, he was employed at the Riverton Lock in Colbert County. At the time of my birth, Dad was employed by Sid Johnson as a carpenter during the construction of St. James Methodist. (My dear 17- year-old mother dedicated me to the Lord through the rites of Christian Baptism when the new brick Church was completed.)

Our home was on Minnehaha Street in East Florence at the time of my birth. (Mrs. Thatcher was the mid-wife who delivered me.) Our next door neighbor was Frank Rickard, Dad's first cousin. Cousin Mary was a small child when her mother died not long after my birth. Grandpa McDonald and Uncle Alphonse were living with us when I arrived. (They waited on the footbridge below the house while I was coming in to the world.) When I was about six months old, Mother caught Grandpa McDonald introducing me to Scottish whiskey with a teaspoon.

Following the completion of St. James, Dad was unemployed. One can imagine his joy when Sid Johnson called him to Cape Cod, Massachusetts, to work on the Buzzard Bay Canal. Mother and I lived with her parents on Staunton Avenue in East Florence while Dad was up north. Uncle Nelson and Uncle Howard became my daddy while we lived there. Uncle Marvin and Claud were playmates. All of my uncles seemed more like brothers, even after we were grown. (For many years the only two Christmas cards we received each year were from Sid Johnson and Cecil Holt. I looked forward each Christmas to their arrival.)

Brother Joe was born soon after Dad returned to Alabama. We had moved to Sweetwater Avenue in a rental house next door to Great-Aunt Maggie Cole. (This was one of Great-Grandpa Johnson's houses.) Aunt Maggie made a little "Ragged Ann" doll for me. I called it "Donna." Aunt Effie took me to town on the streetcar and I carried Donna along in my arms.

Uncle Hardy Springer helped Dad find a job with Shell Oil. Dad and his Negro helper installed gas pumps for service stations throughout Lauderdale, Colbert, and Franklin counties. We lived in a house on Royal Avenue, about two doors from the North Florence Cotton Gin. Uncle Hardy, Aunt Carmel, and Cousin Raymond Glenn lived in two rooms and we had the two rooms nearer the gin. I'll long remember the humming of the cotton gin. Another recollection is standing in the window on a snowy morning watching Dad as he dug his oil truck from a deep snow. (Shell Oil had modified an old Buick hearse for him to use.)

Dad's first cousin, Clarence McDonald, employed Dad to drive one of his buses. We moved again, this time to Sweetwater Avenue next door to Great-Aunt Lottie. Her husband, Rob Lindsey, who was mother's cousin, died while we lived there. Uncle Rob farmed Patton Island. Late in the day when he came in, he would stop the wagon and call "Little Willie Wooden Leg." This was my signal to climb on the wagon and ride to the barn. On occasions, Dad would take me with him on his bus trip to Haleyville. We stopped by the post office to pick up mail for Haleyville. Our trip would include picking up large barrels of ice cream packed in dry ice for delivery to drugstores in Russellville and Haleyville. Every day an elderly gentleman name "Little" rode with is. I wondered if Littleville was named for him. Dan was born while we lived on Sweetwater Avenue.

The Depression began closing in on us. Cousin Clarence had to cut back and eventually close his bus runs. My Daddy was a hard worker. Losing his job was especially difficult. I remember greeting him at the door with an anxious question: "Did you find a job today, Daddy?" One day he lined up with other jobless applicants at the knitting mill to bid on a short- term project called "scaling the boiler." One had to work inside the large cylinder almost without ventilation while he chipped away the rust with a hammer and chisel. When Dad was asked if he had any experience he replied "No." The foreman said "Why do you think I would hire you with no experience?" Dad replied, "Because I'm going to bid half of the amount these other fellows will work for."

Dad said that this was the hardest task he had ever done. Bob Pounders was our landlord. He had no mercy. We were not able to pay the rent. There was no place to go. I remember on a summer day, Dad by some means brought home a watermelon. As we ere eating it on our back porch, we saw Mr. Pounders heading toward our house. Dad hurriedly gathered all the pieces of the watermelon and I crawled under the house to hide them.

It was late summer when Dad bought two tents for less than $20. Great-Aunt Lottie allowed us to place these tents on her back lot between her house and barn. Actually, the tents were fastened to wooden walls which measured about four feet in height. The main tent was floored with planks nailed to two-by-fours placed on the ground. This was our sleeping quarters. Mother and Dan slept on the bed. Dad slept on the floor with Joe and me. We had a pot-belly stove in which we burned short cuts of wood. The other tent had no floor. It was our kitchen. Cousin Frank Rickard gave us a cook stove. Dad made our table and benches from planks left over from flooring the main tent. Curtains were used to provide privacy for Grandpa McDonald who slept in one corner of the kitchen tent.

The only furniture we managed to save, other than one bed and chair, were two wicker chairs and a wicker couch. They were Mother's prized possessions. Dad hid them in the barn. I recall how Mother cried the morning we learned that someone had taken them.

Fetching water was my chore. Our drinking water came from a faucet attached to a water line that carried portable water from Gray Spring to the Cherry Cotton Mill. This outlet was perhaps a distance of a city block from our tents.

Our wash water came from a wet weather spring in a ditch near the tents. There were times when I had to fill the water buckets after nightfall. I saw all kinds of ghosts and panthers as I ran back to the tents spilling water all over my pants. Now and then Dad would go with me. I thought him to be the bravest man in the whole world. It snowed a lot during my first year at school. Mother kept me at home on those days because I had no coat and there were holes in my shoes. Miss Bowsley was my teacher. She called me to the front to explain why I had missed so many days. When I explained to the class that I did not have a coat and had holes in my shoes, they laughed. Miss Bowsley then marched up and slapped me so hard that I could not hear for days afterwards.

Dad explained to Joe and me that Santa would not be able to find us in a tent. On Christmas morning, Cousin Nathan Rickard came to show us his red wagon. He let us ride in it. On the night before Christmas Eve, Mother sent Joe and me to St. James Methodist Church. That was the biggest Christmas tree I had ever seen. During the service, Santa came in and passed out presents to all the children. He did not call our names. Joe cried all the way back to our tents.

Dad built a two-wheel cart. He and I and Cousin Dewey would cut stumps in the wood yard. We hauled these stumps back to our place and split them into what we called stove wood. Occasionally we sold a cart of stove wood, sometimes for eggs or butter. We were never hungry. After I left home I learned from Cecil Holt, the local grocer, that Dad had made an agreement with him to carry us until he found work. Cecil told Uncle Clyde Carter many years after the depression that Ervin McDonald was the most honest man he had ever known. Dad repaid Cecil for every morsel of food we ate during the bleak depression years.

When I entered the Army I could hardly believe all the good food! While most of my comrades complained about the food, I gained more than thirty pounds in basic training.

President-elect Franklin D. Roosevelt came to the Muscle Shoals on January 21, 1933. Dad held me on his shoulders as the greatest man on earth passed by. The TVA Act was signed soon afterwards and Dad was called to work in November.

Daddy quickly bought a house, paying a little over $400 for four rooms, no electricity, and no water closets. But it was a mansion! Bobby, Sis, John, and Tom were born here. The depression did not go away until World War II began. Dad built a one-room house in our backyard for Uncle Alphonse and his family. Later, Uncle Carlos lived here. Finally, Dad dismantled it and used the lumber to build a kitchen to our home.

Dad and Cousin Frank bought a 267 acre farm a few miles south of Collinwood. We built a three-room log house. Cousin Hunter and Cousin Minnie lived there. One Thanksgiving I was there alone cutting wood. The axe slipped and cut a deep gash in my hand. I ran down the hollow until I found an old lady who packed my hand in soot from her fireplace. This stopped the bleeding. I entered the Army when I was 18. I came back on leave and was married to the prettiest girl in Florence. Thus, begins a new chapter of my life in a new home. There is a gospel hymn that says, "I Wouldn't Take Nothing For My Journey Now."

Appendix 7 – Photo Gallery

Adrian L. Lindsey, Sr.,
Company C, 27th Alabama
Infantry CSA

This is 'Mamma Lindsey' as I knew her. She was my mother's mother and lived two houses from us. She died October 30, 1951 when I was six years old. (Tom McDonald)

This photo shows the homeplace built by Franklin Pierce Johnson and his wife Mary Ellender McCuan Johnson. It stood on Sweetwater Avenue in East Florence at the foot of the hill where our house was located. It was a landmark for the community for as long as it stood. Pappy Johnson built the structure in the late 1800s, and it was torn down after the death of his youngest daughter, Effie, in 1968. When I was a child, it was occupied by Aunt Maggie and Aunt Effie. It has been a beehive of activity for all the Johnsons, Lindseys, and McDonalds for many decades. I have many fond memories of parking my bike on the front sidewalk and talking with my great-aunts on the front porch. This picture includes six of eight children. A son, Fred, drowned in the spring behind the house when he was less than two years old, and the youngest daughter, Effie, are not pictured. Beginning in the lower left hand corner, Aunt Maggie, third from the left, is pictured with two of her sons, Claude and Louie. Standing to her right is her brother Robert McCuan Johnson. To Robert's immediate right is the father of the clan, Franklin Pierce Johnson (Pappy) with his daughter Freddie (named after her deceased younger brother, Fred) by his side. Seated to the right of Freddie is their mother, Mary Ellender McCuan Johnson (Mammy). Behind Mammy is her son, George Elliott Johnson. Standing beside George Elliott is Lucy Lavinia Johnson (my grandmother) and her brother Roscoe is next to her. Martha Nichols Johnson (Pappy Johnson's mother) is seated in front of Roscoe. (Tommy McDonald)

Martha Nichols Johnson, 1827-1908. Great-great-grandmother of the McDonald children on their mother's side.

Franklin Pierce Johnson and his wife Mary Ellender
McCuan Johnson (center) with their oldest child,
Magnolia Johnson Cole.

From Left: Effie Johnson, her sister Maggie Johnson
Cole and Maggie's granddaughter Evelyn.

Maggie: 1874-1962   Effie: 1903-1968

Leonard and Lucy Lindsey, grandparents of the author, with their oldest child, Carmel. Lucy and Leonard were married November 9, 1902. Carmel married Hardy R. Springer and was called 'Sister Springer' by her nieces and nephews. This photograph was probably made in 1904.

Leonard and Lucy Lindsey with their youngest child, Mary Ellen. This picture was made in the early 1930s.

Papa Lindsey as I remember him. He is shown with one of his daughter Lura's children. My earliest memories of 'Papa' include him raising chickens, selling eggs and running a small store out of the front of his home. He died May 30, 1960. This photo was made in the late 1950's. (Tom McDonald)

Mary Ellen Lindsey

Nelson Lindsey and his sister
Pauline, mother of the authors.

Howard Lindsey with his
mother

Lura Lindsey, aunt of the authors.

Carmel Lindsey, Pauline Lindsey, and Carlos Lindsey. This picture was made in 1910.

Nelson Lindsey with his wife, Mary.

Pauline Lindsey, Helen Carter, Ludell Parrish, Louise Milfred, and Lura Lindsey. This picture was made in 1910.

From left back row: Leonard Lindsey, his wife Lucy Johnson Lindsey, youngest daughter Mary Ellen Lindsey. Front Left: granddaughters Mae Virginia Lindsey and her older sister Mary Nell Lindsey. These two sisters are the daughters of Nelson Lindsey. Circa 1950

Mary Ellen Lindsey (1928-1995) on the front porch of our old homeplace in East Florence. Mary Ellen was my mother's sister, the youngest of nine children of Leonard and Lucy Lindsey. In today's educational jargon, Mary Ellen would be labeled mentally retarded. Back then we were just told that Mary Ellen was "slow." She only went to school a few days and spent the remainder of her life with family, friends, and finally a nursing home where she died. She and her parents lived only two houses away from us and she spent most of her time at our house. My mother felt a special obligation to care for her. After the death of her parents, Mary Ellen lived with us until my mother died in 1964. She had three great loves in her life: her family, rocking chairs and a porch swing. Unlike most people I know, Mary Ellen was able to remember the birthday of every member of her family until she died and never failed to remind us of someone's

113

upcoming birthday. She often reminded me of how she rocked me when I was a baby and I remember us spending countless hours swinging on our front porch and singing and laughing. Like most boys, I was bad to pester people and Mary Ellen was a favorite target. In spite of this, we shared many laughs later in life at some of the tricks I pulled on her. While she was living in the nursing home, Mary Ellen would bubble over with excitement when her family visited. She would tell all her friends she was my favorite aunt and I would agree wholeheartedly. Our family made it a practice to gather together on her birthday and special holidays. She never failed to introduce each of us to the staff on each visit. Also, she always insisted that our sister play the piano for the whole nursing home in a sing-a-long. Aunt Mary Ellen was a very special person in the lives of the McDonald Family. Her love for us was far beyond what could be measured. As is the case many times, I was too young and in a hurry to realize the extent of that love and did not take the time to return nearly enough of it. She was a veritable gift from God and I feel blessed that she was a part of my life. (Tommy McDonald)

Pauline Lindsey (author's mother), daughter of Leonard and Lucy Lindsey. Married W.E. McDonald

Lura Lindsey (author's aunt), daughter of Leonard and Lucy Lindsey. Married James F. Hall.

Carlos Lindsey (1907-1974) was the second child born to Leonard and Lucy Lindsey. Carlos was with General Patton's Third Army when they linked with the Russians during WWII. He was highly decorated for heroism while his company was holding a bridge for the army to cross the Rhine River into Germany.

Several Lindseys and McDonalds celebrating Mary Ellen Lindsey's birthday. From left bottom row: unknown boy, Andrea Lindsey, Brenda Lindsey, Katherine Lindsey Haeger, Mary Ellen Lindsey, Johnny McDonald, Bobby McDonald, Virginia McDonald Lindsey. Standing left rear: Bill McDonald, Marvin Lindsey (Mary Ellen's brother) and Tommy McDonald.

Mary Ellen Lindsey, center, pictured with her mother, Lucy Johnson Lindsey on her left, along with several nieces and nephews.

Family of Claud R. Lindsey (son of Leonard and Lucy Lindsey) at Washington D.C., June 7, 1994. Left to right: Eloise Keech Fuller, Patricia Kicker, Mark Lindsey, Marvin Lindsey (Claud's Brother) Lucy Nichols, David Kicker, Claud Lindsey, Jr., W.L. McDonald (author and nephew of Claud)

Pictured are four of the children of Leonard and Lucy Lindsey. From left to right front is son Howard Lindsey and his sister Lura Lindsey Hall. Behind Lura is her brother Marvin Lindsey. Katherine Lindsey Haeger, their niece, is back center. Claud Lindsey is back left.

This picture of William Ervin McDonald and his oldest son Bill, the author, was taken in October, 1945. It was probably taken around the time I was born (Tommy McDonald)

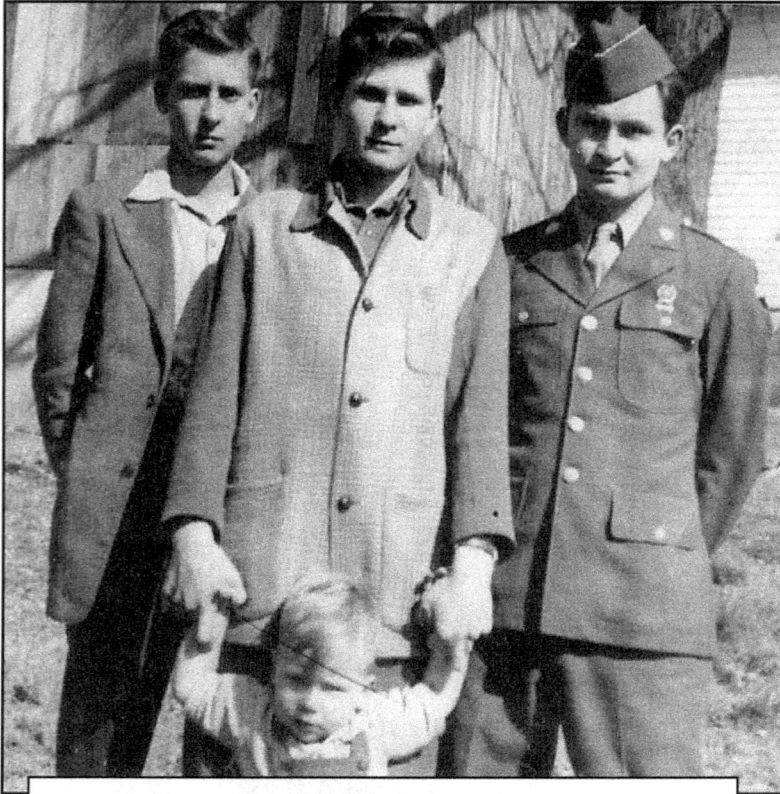

Four of the McDonald brothers from the mid 1940s.

From left standing: Joe McDonald, Dan McDonald and Bill McDonald. Johnny McDonald is the child in front of Dan.

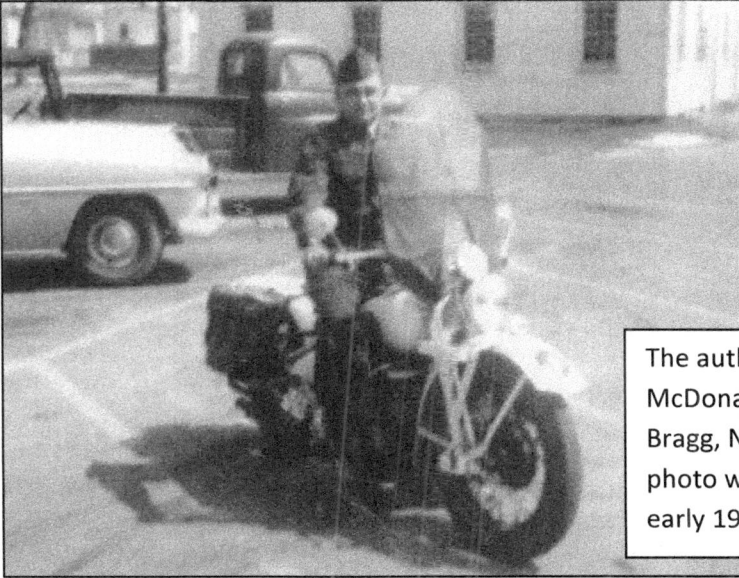

The author, William L. McDonald, as an M.P. at Fort Bragg, North Carolina. This photo was probably made in the early 1950s.

This is our grandfather Jesse William McDonald (1878-1957) as a young man. He was known as 'Pa Mac' by his grandchildren and 'Will Mac' by most everyone else who knew him. He had piercing blue eyes and always carried a pocket watch in his vest pocket He lived with us and I rarely saw him out without a dark hat, dark suit and vest. In his later years, he would walk to East Florence from our home and spend most of the day visiting with anyone he happened to come across.
(Tommy McDonald)

Picture at the back of the home place in East Florence. From left rear: Bobby McDonald and Virginia McDonald. Seated from front left: Tommy McDonald and Johnny McDonald. This photo was probably made in 1948.

This mid 1950s photo shows three generations of the McDonald family. From left standing: Jesse William McDonald (grandfather), Joe McDonald, Bobby McDonald, Bill McDonald. Front row from left standing: Tommy McDonald, Virginia McDonald William Ervin McDonald (father), Pauline McDonald (mother), and Johnny McDonald.

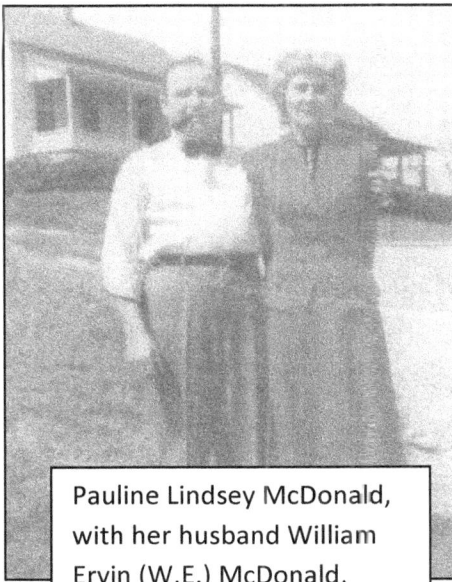

Pauline Lindsey McDonald, with her husband William Ervin (W.E.) McDonald.

Pauline Lindsey McDonald

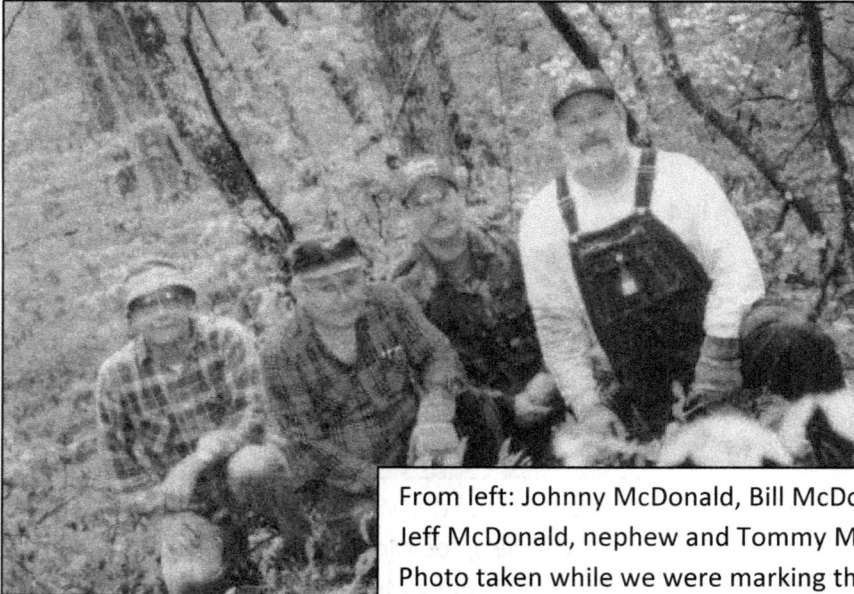

From left: Johnny McDonald, Bill McDonald, Jeff McDonald, nephew and Tommy McDonald. Photo taken while we were marking the graves of several relatives in the Higgins Cemetery near Waterloo, AL on April 12, 1997.

William Ervin McDonald, center, being pestered by sons Joe, left and Bobby, right.

The author, far right, and several brothers at the wedding of Joe McDonald's granddaughter in Athens, Alabama. From left: Bobby McDonald , Tommy McDonald, Johnny McDonald, Joe McDonald and Bill McDonald.

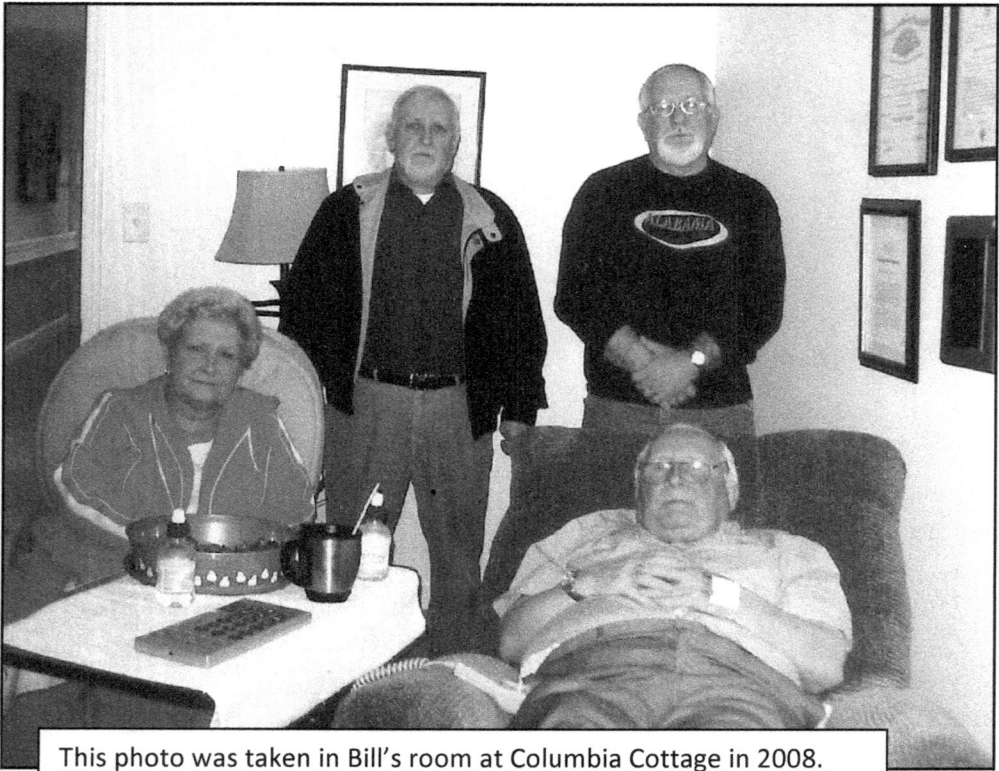

This photo was taken in Bill's room at Columbia Cottage in 2008. From left: Sister Virginia Lindsey, brother Joe McDonald, brother Tom McDonald and Bill McDonald in front.

Index

T

Published by

Bluewater Publications is a multi-faceted publishing company capable of meeting all of your reading and publishing needs. Our two-fold aim is to:

1) Provide the market with educationally enlightening and inspiring research and reading materials and to
2) Make the opportunity of being published available to any author and or researcher who so desires to become published.

We are passionate about preserving history; whether it is through the re-publishing of an out-of-print classic or by publishing the research of historians and genealogists, Bluewater Publications is the publisher you need.

To learn more about the Dr. William Lindsey McDonald or for information about how you can be published through Bluewater Publications, please visit:

www.BluewaterPublications.com

Confidently Preserving Our Past,

Bluewater Publications.com

Formerly Known as Heart of Dixie Publishing

www.ingramcontent.com/pod-product-compliance
Lightning Source LLC
Chambersburg PA
CBHW081155270326
41930CB00014B/3161